Grimsby
The Story of the World's Greatest Fishing Port

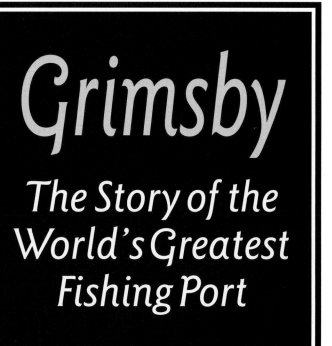

Grimsby

The Story of the World's Greatest Fishing Port

Peter Chapman

breedon **books**
PUBLISHING

First published in Great Britain in 2002 by
The Breedon Books Publishing Company Limited
Breedon House, 3 The Parker Centre,
Derby, DE21 4SZ.

ISBN 1 85983 323 3

Printed and bound by Butler & Tanner, Frome, Somerset,
England.

Cover printing by Lawrence-Allen Colour Printers, Weston-
super-Mare, Somerset, England.

CONTENTS

In memory of Kenneth Sleight (RAFVR), Alan 'Sandy' Croft Baker (RNR), H. 'Ticker' Sproston (RAF), Huntley Goude (King's Own Yorkshire Light Infantry), Sydney Croft Baker (Merchant Navy), Roland Goodwin (Royal Artillery), and Rodger Doig (The Black Watch), who gave their lives in the service of their country and who were part of my life.

ACKNOWLEDGEMENTS

This book is elaborated by some excellent photographs, many unfamiliar to you.

Principal among those who had the perspicacity to take them is the late Harold Hillam (1906–1981), a Grimsby schoolmaster who taught at both Nunsthorpe School from its inception in 1931 and, later at Chelmsford School.

He supplemented his income with commercial work, weddings, amateur theatricals, portraiture and so on. But there was a latent newspaperman in him and he took exceptional pictures en passant.

During World War Two he served with SOE at Welwyn.

I am also grateful to other, nameless photographers of yore and to a variety of friends, among them the Borough Archivist John Wilson, Peter Green of Irby and Group Captain Alan Hollingsworth, to the *Evening Telegraph's* Linda Roberts and her several computer literate friends, to my Godmother at North Thoresby and to those who have nudged me in one direction or another, old colleagues or old friends all.

I apologise to my wife Annie. I have had my head in a book for the last time.

CHRONICLES

THERE have been several histories of Grimsby. Of the six with which you will be most familiar, *The Monumental Antiquities of Grimsby*, published in 1825 by Dr (of divinity) George Oliver, is reliable and is often quoted by his successors. Dr Oliver was, at the time and for 17 years, Vicar of Clee and his book was printed in Hull. In a largely illiterate Grimsby it would not have been widely read, indeed the subscribers' list reveals his audience. Phrases like 'druidical polytheism' were above most people's heads then, as now. In 1866 however – and having become Rector of South Hykeham – he decided to popularise his first, earnest book and published, in Grimsby, the extraordinary *Ye Byrde of Gryme*, a history of the town relayed to the reader via the beak of a long-lived raven.

'Do you believe me to be an honest man?' he asked in his preface. 'If not then throw my book in the fire. If so I beseech you to place implicit faith in the contents of this little volume.'

Many found the fire a handy target. Ever since 1866, scorn has been heaped on *Ye Byrde*.

But however fanciful – Oliver suggests Shakespeare came here and wrote *Hark, Hark the Lark at heaven's gate sings* – it is a whimsy which sought to popularise an interest in the town's past for the ever-growing population of complete strangers arriving in it.

In 1893 the Grimsby solicitor Anderson Bates (of Bates and Mountain) and a protegé of William Heaford Daubney, published a delightful melange of memories and nostalgia, *A Gossip About Old Grimsby*, vignette-like chapters before memory

The Revd George Shaw, historian of the 1890s.

dimmed, of a long-gone Georgian town and the characters who lived in it. Unpretentious and not at all dry, it is a reliable reference work written by a man at the very heart of the town's affairs. Bates died in 1899, aged 75.

Edward Gillett, Borough Archivist, historian of modern times.

Two years before he died, the Revd George Shaw published his *Old Grimsby*. By 1897, Grimsby was in need of an up-to-date history and Shaw, a prominent Primitive Methodist minister, produced, in old age, a very workmanlike book which relied heavily on Dr Oliver. Shaw, who also started his working life in W.H. Daubney's office, died in 1903 aged 72. His wife survived him until 1921.

Grimsby's next – and probably best known – chronicler was the ebullient Bob Lincoln, a painter and decorator turned builder who went to print in 1913 with his enormous tour-de-force *The Rise of Grimsby,* with the County Borough crest proudly stamped on the front cover. Many – too many – objecting and objectionable comments have been made about Bob Lincoln's contribution. Of course, it is possible to find fault in both volumes. Pendantry thrives now as years ago.

Lincoln was not of the teetotal, Nonconformist, Liberal persuasion and the hearty public-bar jargon shines through on almost every page. He did not disguise his opinions.

Relying heavily on what had gone before for his early and medieval chapters, he comes into his own in the second volume which is a well observed and highly detailed portrait of Grimsby emerging – as Dr Oliver said – 'from the chrysalis state in which she vegetated for years and is now assuming the golden butterfly'.

Lincoln, whose death in 1918 was hastened by the death of his son in the RFC during the war, was a Grimsby man through and through, full of pontoon humour, a local celebrity, sportsman and raconteur. He wrote his history not out of a desire to educate, but because he loved his home town.

Gratitude was the reason the Revd Moses Davies,

The irrepressible Bob Lincoln (1856–1918), cricketer, builder, recorder of his times.

Anderson Bates (1824–1899) solicitor, prominent freemason and historian.

Vicar of Ravendale, wrote his *The History of Grimsby* which was published, remarkably enough, in the middle of World War Two. A Welshman, Davies was, in 1942, aged 62 and had been at Ravendale for 17 years. His book is an expansion of a lecture to Grimsby Rotary Club which he was urged to put into print by Harold King and Dr John Cotterill. Davies, who regretted that Grimsby did not have a museum and deplored its Philistinism, added little to our understanding. But his book filled a gap.

The town's last historian was Edward Gillett, appointed honorary archivist to the Grimsby Corporation in 1952 (when L.W. Heeler was town clerk). His *A History of Grimsby* was published in 1969. With the exception of Oliver's first book, this is the only study of the town by an academic and is both thorough and reliable and more than amply bolstered by source references, copious notes, appendices and so on.

Gillett was either helped or hindered – according to your point of view – by not being a local man.

There have been many books, booklets, pamphlets alluding to Grimsby and aspects of its life and the conjoint life of its near neighbour, Cleethorpes.

The Revd Frank Baker (1953), George Lester (1890), The Revd C. Ernest Watson (1901), Richard Mason, Daphne and Leon Gerlis, Charles Ekberg and so on wrote on local Methodism, local fishing and other matters. All had perspectives.

Yet few of the 19th-century books would have been of more than passing interest to those living in Grimsby. Indeed, a book on Barking or Brixham might have found a substantial readership for, by 1890, the enormously increased and fast increasing population were not natives at all but had arrived here in their tens of thousands – artisans, professionals and the semi-qualified with but one ambition – to earn a living.

It mattered not a jot to anyone of them that Grimsby had a past of any description and, to those who could read and were even slightly interested in the billet they had found on the East Coast, Grimsby's history seemed larded with myth and legend and supposition and speculation.

We are now in a new century and the people who made Grimsby great – or recreated Great Grimsby – have left the stage. Little vestige of them remains.

Motives and passions have flared and died, and fervour – social, religious, military and commercial – has run its course.

Grimsby was a phenomenon, a town which happened. Its constituent families, with all their determination, involvement, bravery, generosity of spirit and pride in the town they made, have moved on.

This book is about them and their vanished past. It is not a profound book. I do not have the scholarship.

GENESIS

A<small>T THE</small> end of the 18th century, Grimsby had been remaindered. Miles from anywhere, its sole contact with the outside world coming from sporadic visits from the mail coach, its population had sunk to little over 900. One of the known causes of death was starvation. An insignificant riverside village, by-passed by great events – particularly the Industrial Revolution – its further decline was arrested only by a group of rural grandees who, seeking to enhance their fortunes,

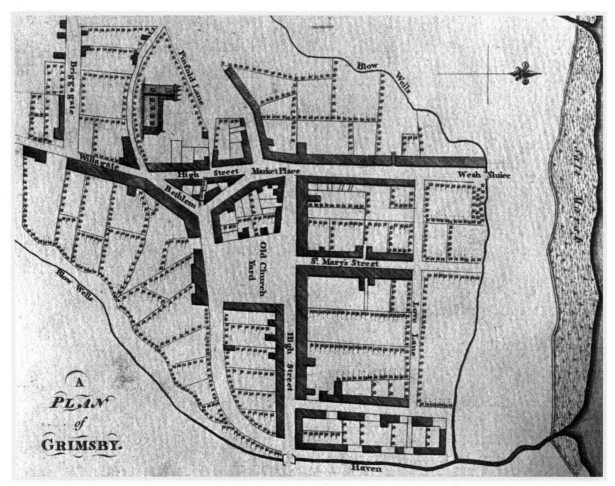

This stylised map of the late 18th century reveals Grimsby as it was before the railways came... small, compact, medieval and with the space (centre) where once had stood St Mary's Church. It is part of the Armstrong Survey of 1789.

formed a company to excavate Grimsby's silted-up dock and make fresh access to the Humber.

The story of the Grimsby Haven Company is both fascinating and well-documented. I refer the reader immediately to Gordon Jackson's comprehensive *Grimsby and the Haven Company 1796–1846*. No account of the company's life could be bettered.

For a multiplicity of reasons the Haven Company failed, as did other attempts to breath life into the corpse – notably, whaling. But in the 1840s, a decade of railway company exploration, the moribund port of Grimsby was seen by the chairman of the Manchester, Sheffield and Lincolnshire Railway Company, John Chapman, as an asset beyond price.

The view, although prophetic, was scarcely shared. Chapman, however, insisted that his company should extend its rail network much further than Gainsborough (its initial target) and press on to Grimsby and acquire the dormant rights of the old Haven Company. Thus, briefly, the railway came to town, its lines entering from the west, its passenger station just behind the Market Place, hub of what there was of Grimsby.

Then, directly, and across open, barren, sedge-tufted marshland-fitties, the lines ran straight to the river's edge so that the company's trucks could bring the wherewithal for the building of a dock. And there the lines stopped.

The construction of the Royal Dock, necessitating the reclamation of about 140 acres of the unpredictable Humber, began in 1846 and involved massive piling and draining before Prince Albert, Victoria's consort, could lay the foundation stone in 1849. Work on the 20-acre dock then proceeded apace, one of its two lock entrances made 70ft wide

to admit the largest of the Royal Navy's warships. However, this eye-to-a-customer was not to result in the specific rewards intended.

The lock gates were operated by hydraulic mechanism dependent on a 33,000-gallon water tank housed in an enormous 300ft tower. They are no longer so operated. But the tower became, and remains, the very symbol of Grimsby.

The Royal Dock, which opened for business in May 1852 and the initial basic provision of a primitive fish dock had cost the MS & L £1 million. Would the investment pay dividends? Not for nothing was the MS & L initially, and fearfully, known as the Money Sunk and Lost. But a dock is an end in itself. It does not require industries to support it. It is a conduit. It allows for both exports and imports and the levying of charges for both. The subsequent revenue would eventually pay for the investment, and dividends to both directors and shareholders.

From this dynamic start, two towns emerged. The first was the old inland Grimsby, its street pattern quite unchanged since medieval times, its core St James's Church, its buildings insignificant, mean, no more than one storey high, its Town Hall small.

The new, some two miles distant, was a noisy thriving shambles, its workforce Irish immigrants, its ambition international trade involving the prosperity of Sheffield and Belgium, Manchester and the Baltic, places far removed from old Grimsby.

The existing 'powers' in Grimsby were in the old town and were, more specifically, in two offices, both solicitor's premises. In one sat William Grange. In the other William Heaford

William Grange, Grimsby's (and Britain's) longest-lived town clerk.

William Heaford Daubney, solicitor, agent for Sidney Sussex College, Cambridge, the man who oversaw the development of New Clee.

Daubney. Both were country lawyers, Grange Grimsby's *de facto* town clerk, Daubney the representative on the ground of landed estates whose proprietors lived elsewhere. Neither was overwhelmed by the sudden transformation of their fiefdom into a burgeoning inter-continental port.

And when John Chapman stood down as chairman of the MS & L, his place was taken by a true giant of Victorian England, a man who was to transform Grimsby and make it his own, private, bride. His name was Edward Watkin.

He, through his company, decided what the town's future was to be, what its requirements were and when things should be done. And how. Watkin, for 40 years, exerted a hold on the town which amounted to a benevolent dictatorship. Little happened without the approval of, and at the instigation of, his company.

Watkin virtually appointed Grimsby's Members of Parliament, not caring what their politics were just so long as they were 'company men'. He saw himself as 'Mr Grimsby' and said openly that he had made the fortunes of everyone in town ...and had made the town itself.

There was a lot of truth in it and none to deny it. There was much fawning. Although an MP himself (for Folkestone), Edward Watkin placed his company and its commercial interests far above politics and, through every means from coercion to blatant nepotism, left no room for doubt that without him Grimsby would be nothing, and that it was he who held the town's development in his hands.

Edward William Watkin, a businessman's son, was born in Manchester on 26 September 1819 and became fascinated with railways and their potential. Leaving his father's business he became, in 1845, secretary to the Trent Valley Railway Company. After a brief association with the London & North-Western he began his long service with the MS & L, first as general manager, then company secretary and company director and, finally and for years, chairman.

He was, further, chairman of the South-Eastern, director of the Great Western and the Great Eastern and the president of the Grand Trunk Railway of Canada. He stood for Parliament at the age of 38, became MP for Stockport and, later, for Hythe and Folkestone. He might as well have been MP for Grimsby. And although he never was, he remedied the situation as soon as he could.

Political factions interested him not at all. He changed sides with the wind, sometimes a Tory, sometimes a Liberal and always in the interests of the railway companies with which he was associated. It was remarkable, wrote a contemporary, how he found time both for the Commons and the railway company boardrooms. He was passionate about tunnels. The Channel Tunnel had no greater protagonist... nor indeed a plan for a Humber tunnel, or even one linking Scotland with the north of Ireland. In tunnelling alone he was frustrated. But in nothing else. He was knighted in 1868, became High

Sir Edward Watkin, the man who transformed Grimsby. Apart from his railway interests, Sir Edward began to build at Wembley a rival to the Eiffel Tower, on the site of the later Empire Stadium.

Sheriff of his native Cheshire in 1874 and was made a baronet in 1880. He died in April 1901.

But his successors in the MS & L chairman's seat, Lord Wharncliffe, and later, Sir Alexander Henderson, were not the single-minded patrons of Grimsby to which the town had become accustomed. Only then did Grimsby realise to whom it was really beholden. Under Watkin's supervision the town had been transformed from a muddy Georgian wilderness into an international Victorian success. In truth Sir Edward Watkin had had little with which to contend.

From the beginning, Grimsby town council, and its guiding lights the solicitors Grange and Daubney, were compliant, frequently powerless to do anything other than what Watkin and the MS & L required of them. Old Grimsby was in thrall. However it may seem at this distance in time, it was not a bad thing. To survive, Grimsby had required being taken by the scruff of the neck and knocked into shape. For without a new master it would have languished.

The piper, of course, had to be paid. If the company gave, then the company expected to receive. Requests were seldom denied and, when they were, cost the town dear. The company, in the laying of tracks, the acquisition of land, the excavating of docks, the building of warehouses and wharves, invested millions in their new-found town.

They negotiated cleverly, establishing the right, in 1869, to buy what land they might require in the future at 1869 prices – no matter how many years had elapsed. And when, five years later, they required 100 acres of the West Marsh for the cutting of the Union Dock and the later building of the Alexandra Dock, they made their £300-per-acre offer. The council demurred. The company told them to take it or leave it. The council took it.

The company did the town and its people favours. When plans for a footbridge linking Newmarket Street with the Central Market were required, the railway company provided them free of charge. In 1874, after having built a railway line to Cleethorpes – thus making the resort a fait accompli – the company built a high wall along the frontage with Stirling Street and Harrington Street. But the smack skippers who lived there could then no longer see the river and their returning fishing boats. They complained. At some considerable expense the company kindly lowered the height of the wall by several feet.

However when, in 1872, a railway company-owned fish dock refreshment room was refused a drinks licence – after suggestions by teetotal smack owners that their crews were being led astray by alcoholic blandishments – there was indignation. An immediate appeal was made. Needless to say the MS & L won the appeal. It cost Grimsby Corporation £113.

So it was that what the company wanted the company obtained, leavening its demands by largesse, the latter gratefully received. It seemed both churlish in view of the benefits – and foolish in view of the long odds – to oppose it. And the compromises were not too hard to bear.

The company consolidated its position in many ways.

John Sutcliffe, the pioneering shipping agent who died in Grimsby in 1877 was the shipping and forwarding agent specifically for the MS & L.

John Fildes, MP from 1865 to 1868, was the father-in-law of John Wintringham who was William Grange's partner. And when, in 1875, the grid-pattern West Marsh residential estate was laid out, William Grange personally designed that layout, and streets were named after John Fildes, John Chapman, Lord Annesley, Lord Yarborough and, of course, Sir Edward Watkin, railway company men all.

It would be wrong to suggest that Watkin transformed the town entirely alone. It would also be wrong to suggest that Grange and Daubney were trembling lackeys at his feet. They formed, as far as local affairs were concerned, a triumvirate. Grange who lived to be 91 – thus becoming the oldest town clerk in England – died in office. His life spanned the Grimsby renaissance. His surname survives in his old firm, Grange and Wintringham. His was an age which embraced the stage coach – Grimsby was served by at least four – and the motor car. The railway, which was to dominate his life, was the interim transport measure.

Grange, it was, who supervised the transference of the powers and clout of the old Haven Company. In doing so, incidentally, the £100 shares of the Haven Company (which had fallen in value to just £5) were immediately restored to the status quo ante.

Daubney, Grange's senior by three years, was born in Grimsby in 1816 and, at the age of 21, became agent for Sidney Sussex College, Cambridge, principal Clee and Cleethorpes landowners, an office his father had held before him. He was, during 1847–8 and again 1851–2 mayor of Grimsby and was, like Grange intimately bound up with the progressive affairs of the town.

In the interests of the town – including New Clee, then a hinterland of fitties – both men bent with the wind in wholesome municipal interest. The link between Top Town legislature and railway company progress was much assisted by the Member of Parliament.

In 1875 John Fildes died in Manchester. He was a stockbroker with a special interest in railway undertakings. In 1877 John Chapman, MP from 1862–5, both before and again after Fildes, was the former chairman of the MS & L and the very man who had brought the railway to Grimsby.

And Chapman was also the man who negotiated with the Great Northern Railway which resulted in the Grimsby-Louth-Peterborough-London being allowed to use the MS & L's 'facilities', notably town station. In addition he virtually paid for the artillery volunteers' barracks in Victoria Street. But more of that later.

Colonel George Tomline, England's richest commoner, Grimsby's absentee MP.

Between Fildes and Chapman came the exceptional Colonel George Tomline, the wealthiest commoner in Britain, allegedly Grimsby's worst MP (due to his absenteeism) when the town was said to be totally unrepresented in Parliament – a state of affairs which suited the railway company admirably.

In 1877 the railway company almost exceeded its self-appointed brief when Edward Watkin fielded his own son as Parliamentary candidate. There was serious trouble. Young Watkin – Alfred Mellor Watkin – was considered a complete duffer. The riot at the Royal Hotel during the election campaign is part of Grimsby's well documented past. Young Watkin could not string two words together and even apologised for being nothing much of a speaker. But his father had, by this time, ensured that Grimsby was in the railway company's pocket and it mattered not a jot to him what politics were involved or who the candidate was, just so long as the man returned was a company man.

'I think the company should keep control of the Borough,' said Sir Edward.

Young Watkin was elected, a company man returned. That was all that mattered. The fighting at the Royal Hotel involving stair rods, fire irons, stones, police from Hull, arrests, just did not matter.

In 1880 Edward Heneage was first elected MP for Grimsby. A railway company director, he was making a fortune by allowing his adjacent and encroaching farmland to become developed, affording welcome relief from the farming depression of the late 19th century. At the peak of the building on the the Heneage Estates in Grimsby he was earning at least £6,000 a year as ground landlord. Heneage was also, and for good reason, a great protagonist of the fishing industry.

Sir Edward Watkin's last 'appointed' MP was the French exile Henri Josse, at the time of his election the most popular man in town. Josse was entirely Watkin's protege. Watkin had long before decided to add coal exporting to Grimsby's tally of trades. Josse, a political refugee, had come here in the 1850s specifically to mastermind coal exports and, by 1877

was despatching 313,000 tons annually, and all to France. Despite being unable to master English, Josse became very wealthy indeed, joined the town council, was appointed a JP and was extravagantly supported by Sir Edward Watkin.

Although Josse was a Liberal and Sir Edward, at that time, a Tory, Watkin virtually got him into Parliament and provoked a bitter row in Westminster. Tories should not, it was felt, promote Liberals. But Josse was a company man. The effort, sad to say, killed Josse within a year of his election. Heneage came back to fill the void.

Josse's death marked the end of the Watkin sway – the Watkin 'management' of Grimsby ...for good or bad. But it had been for good. Daubney, speaking for everyone with a commercial interest in Grimsby – and there was no other interest so important – said openly: 'I believed in the enterprising genius of Sir Edward Watkin. It may be doubted whether any man has conferred greater or more signal benefit on any town than the chairman of the MS & L.' It was not doubted by any man.

And Daubney knew that, by 1879, Sidney Sussex College was deriving a quarter of its income from development at New Clee, that income rising, by 1900, to half of its total. At his death Sir Edward was declared in a Gladstonian reference to be the Grand Old Man of railways. He was, said an obituarist, 'endowed with the courage of his convictions but was vain, impetuous and capricious'. Grimsby people were able to forgive him all that.

And then there was fish. Fish and fishing were not incidentals – or accidentals – on the agenda of the MS & L. But they could be described as bonuses.

The Royal Dock, after all, was not ideal for fishing smacks. But a combination of factors was, ultimately, to result in fishing eclipsing the Royal Dock's importance. The discovery of magnificent fishing grounds in the North Sea was allied to an obscure dispute in Hull (which concerned dock dues). The opportunist directors of the railway company, led by Chapman, inspired inducements to the Hull men to land their catches and transfer their ships to

John Brown, born at Irby in 1815, died at 10 St James' Terrace, Bargate, Grimsby in June 1892, the man who built the first prominent buildings in Grimsby. His considerable fortune was harnessed post-mortem in the fishing industry.

the Barking, the Kent, the Yorkshire (and eventually the Norfolk) coasts. The Barking and Kent areas were suffering particularly from the increased sewage effluent from the ever-expanding London.

The procession, generally by sea, of smacks and their owners and their wives and children and chattels, grew, and all were welcomed into the maw of the MS & L who then continually improved, improved and improved facilities for them. To accommodate this migration, the hitherto modestly productive tenanted farmland of the Heneages, the Thorolds and especially the sheep-stalked acres of the Sidney Sussex College was built upon, street upon street of sturdy terraced houses, much of it still there.

By 1886, 820 smacks were fishing out of Grimsby. And then came steam power and, following experiments with it, the purpose-built steam trawler. By 1892 there were 799 smacks and 113 steam trawlers. The demise of sail was them dramatic. In 1902, 450 steam trawlers sailed from Grimsby. There were no smacks. In just 10 years the wooden boats became worthless.

Smack owners had decisions to make.

Many gave up the sea and became fish merchants ashore, remaining on the docks. Some abandoned fish entirely and began retail businesses – many of Grimsby's shops starting this way. And there were new industries to be explored, particularly garages. But others – the sea in their blood – banded together in unions bolstered by the banks – especially Smith Ellison's – and founded steam trawling companies. What local money was available, from people like George Doughty and John Brown, builders both, was also harnessed by persuasion.

There was, surprisingly, not much participation by the prosperous timber merchants, the contribution to the fishing industry by their trade being two-fold ...boxmaking for which there was enormous demand, and the provision of shavings and saw dust, which detritus was used in quantity by the fish curing and smoking houses. Waste not want not.

Thus were born trawling companies with high-

Grimsby, and even encouraged it by setting up their own fishing company. Blandishments proved irresistible. By 1852, some 500 tons of fish landed here were being loaded on company trains for consumption miles away. The Royal Dock having indeed proved unsuitable, the company built a proper six-acre dock to the north of it and, by 1863, 10,000 tons of fish were making the inland journeys. The continuing story is well known.

The news of Grimsby's growth spread and other fishermen, endlessly (as today) in search of fish, swelled the numbers from Brixham in Devon, from

Grimsby's original dock – the old dock – became known as the River Head and was the haunt of small boys with fishing rods. In this pre-war study, one of Blow's barges is tied at a quay. Centre are two buoys ashore for repair. The bulk of Marshall's mill rises in the background.

flown titles – the North-Eastern Steam Fishing Company Ltd, the Great Grimsby and East Coast Steam Fishing Company, the Lindsey, the Northwold, the Dolphin, the Orient, the Albion, the Ocean, the Britannia, the Queen, the D-Line and so on, unions all of determined men.

People, of course, used their own names ...Moss, Baskcomb, Jeffs, Taylor, Guzzwell, Osborne, Robinson, Sleight, Green... And there was flattery. Hagerup and Doughty had 'their' company named after them although neither had anything to do with fishing, merely supplying the cash for it.

Employment boomed. Fortunes were in the making. And the word Grimsby began to appear in rather larger and rather bolder type on the map of England.

The Alexandra Dock, eventually the established link between the River Head and, via the Union 'dock', the Royal Dock, was essentially the timber dock. In this 1948 picture the *Jacorus* of Hull unloads her cargo of deal, Marshall's (Spiller's) mill is to the left.

Alderman Dr Thomas Bell Keetley (1821–1890) was extra-typical of the robust and forthright town elders who guided Grimsby to fame in the 19th century. The son of Thomas Keetley, captain of a Greenland whaler, he was not only a surgeon, an alderman, a magistrate and mayor of Grimsby in the 1880s but also a physically strong man who, as a youth, had sailed with his father. In 1875 he set about a well-known Grimsby troublemaker and floored him in a 'three-round' contest on Grimsby Town railway station platform. 'This is not the first time a man has felt the force of Dr Keetley's fists,' reported a local newspaper (*Grimsby Observer*).

But it was the great Royal Dock, dominated by the tower modelled on the Campanile in Siena, which established Grimsby. The tower incidentally, some 309ft high, was completed in 1854 and is the work of the architect James William Wild (1814–1892). Although a functional piece of engineering, it is a perfect thing, unique in Britain, the symbol of Grimsby and rightly on the cover of Pevsner's Lincolnshire volume.

Many are the early photographs of the Royal Dock when it was packed with sailing ships, merchantment from all over the world, from the US laden with grain, from the Baltic, the South American west coast, Australia. In this study, sail is already giving way to steam. When the wooden sailing ships were broken up their timbers were used by the building trade. Their tufa ballast stones became garden rockeries throughout the town.

Tugs are essential
for all the world's
great harbours
and Grimsby has
had several
companies.

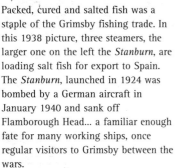

Packed, cured and salted fish was a staple of the Grimsby fishing trade. In this 1938 picture, three steamers, the larger one on the left the *Stanburn*, are loading salt fish for export to Spain. The *Stanburn*, launched in 1924 was bombed by a German aircraft in January 1940 and sank off Flamborough Head... a familiar enough fate for many working ships, once regular visitors to Grimsby between the wars.

The urge to romanticise the life of the working man – and the seaman in particular – has been a constant through the centuries. This superb painting of a barque leaving Grimsby for the North Sea is by J. Edwards and is dated 1898. It is the property of Anthony Carlbom, the well-known local shipping agent. The glamour disguises the uncertain fate of these sturdy, but small, boats.

Although this splendid oil by the celebrated Frank H. Mason (included here by permission of the Royal National Mission to Deep Sea Fishermen) would appear to illustrate 'fleeting' – in which small boats bring their catches to a mother ship – it depicts something altogether more interesting. Entitled *Christmas on the Dogger Bank*, it shows smacks and their boats converging on a larger 'admiral's' smack in order that a Christmas Day church service may be held on board. Smack owners and their skippers were often devout men, mostly of a Low Church persuasion, and the names of their boats frequently reflected their faith.

Fish Dock Road, Grimsby, highway to prosperity.

Top: The art nouveau cartouche framing a gesture to Grimsby fishermen and dated 1899. The men are named, from the left, John Warr, James Wilson and J.W. Steppe.

Bottom: Rather more primitive is this idealised flat-calm view of the entrances to the Royal and the Fish Docks;

Going to sea, however, on trawlers in particular, was not a glamorous business, for trawlers do not merely go from A to B but loiter in extremely inclement places, their business to perform. Ice afloat is hazard enough. Ice aboard is a very different matter and a contributing factor to capsizals and losses at sea – and without survivors.

And there, is in truth, nothing enormously attractive about a fisherman's life ashore. Here, the trawler *Viscaria* has her stern tarred by workmen in the most precarious of craft.

Filleting fish – with very sharp knives. Note that the man on the right wears his old army shirt, sergeant's stripes still in place. Injuries to hands were both frequent and terrible. In 1937 Mr Guy Pulvertaft (1907–1986), an orthopaedic consultant, came to Grimsby and stayed for 10 years. In that time he dealt with 10,000 in-patients and 20,000 out-patients, mostly with hand injuries. He became a specialist in the subject and in hand surgery, won international renown, was awarded the CBE and is recalled for his work on the grafting of flexor tendons in fingers. The gutting knife, while an essential tool, could be a horror.

And the repair of nets is a constant travail...

...as was the splicing of ropes.

And the enormous coal hoists, fuelled by the railway company trucks, were seldom dormant.

Ashore there were ships to mend. In this pre-1914 photograph a group of workmen from Bacon's engineering shops returns from the task in hand.

Horses survived World War Two. Mr R. Moore on the left, the horseman, and his 'nipper lad', E. Croft, then aged 16, were both in LNER employ. Their horse, Jack, used to move individual trucks about. This picture dates from 1934.

Trawlers and fishing boats of all shapes and sizes were what Grimsby depended on. This poignant picture is of the last of the fishing smacks, tied up and worthless in 1903.

In 1938 these two photographs of the pontoon reveal the large numbers of horses on the fish docks, mostly used to pull flat-backed rulleys, four wheeled carts.

The pontoon itself, now largely demolished, was the hub of life for both the fish merchants and the trawler owners. A cold, open-to-all-weathers place, work began very early and sales were generally completed by mid-day. Offices above the sales and gutting areas were reached by spiral cast-iron staircases, the merchants' 'stands' identified by enormous, named, wooden boards.

Typical of the early steam trawlers is the *Orvicto*, one of Sir Thomas Robinson's boats. The wheelhouse is abaft the funnel – not a good arrangement and one which was soon rectified.

Ships became grander and larger. This is the *Galilean*.

And trawlers gave up the use of coal. This is the *Aylesby*, revolutionary in her day.

By 1956 The *Boston Fury* showed the new shape of things... and changed the design of the Fishermen's Friend packet!

And innumerable launches kept their owners... and Grimsby... happy.

For a very brief period, one or two Grimsby trawlers went big game fishing. In the early 1930s, tunny fish, enormous things, 700 or 800lbs in weight, 'visited' the North Sea in quest of herring.

Tunny are game fish and the country's extremely wealthy, among them, for instance Tommy Sopwith, commissioned Grimsby trawlers and their crews to take them into the North Sea... for sport. Here the G.F. Sleight trawler *Renco* GY512, plays host to an enthusiast in 1933... and the result, which dwarfs Colonel Richard Sparrow CMG DSO former CO of the 7th Dragoon Guards. It was clearly worth all the effort – and expense. The tunny fishing ended as abruptly as it had started. It is barely recalled.

The sort of fish which everyone could enjoy was landed in vast quantity. And despite warnings concerning over-fishing, it continued to be so. One looks at pictures like this with a mix of regret and guilt.

This delightful picture of the North Wall, with the solitary railway company policeman keeping an eye on things, epitomises steady times in pre-war Grimsby.

The sunset over Grimsby fish docks in the late 1930s. How could things ever change?

The final extent of the fish docks, an aerial photograph taken following the opening of the third, and final, dock on 4 October 1934, an extension made possible by the pushing out, and by the construction of the North Wall (right). At the foot of the picture, the coal hoists await completion and rail tracks snake across the wilderness. What a confident sight it all is, and how grateful to the heirs of the Manchester, Sheffield and Lincolnshire Railway everyone must have been. Note too the utterly undeveloped Humber Bank beyond. It was merely a void for things to come.

NUMBERS

PEOPLE came to Grimsby for one reason only – to earn a living. Maybe clergymen would not like to be numbered so. Grimsby was not a seat of learning. Nor was it a garrison town, nor, despite some failed endeavours, did it have naval connections. Nor did it figure large in the Diocese. There was no academy.

But, like its contemporary, the American Wild West, it attracted the determined and very few of the wrong sort. At the end of this brief chapter is a list, not substantial and certainly not all-embracing, of some of the many families and individuals who came here ...and their place of origin.

It is a representative list, people to do with trawling and the fish docks, people in business in its many forms, people in the professions. It is a revealing tally.

A town in the making, like Grimsby, must of necessity import people, doctors for instance, who cannot possibly qualify there, and clergymen and lawyers. But in the mid-19th century Grimsby needed everyone – a substantial working population, a complete artisan class and, ideally, moneyed people. There were none of the latter. Grimsby was to be self-made and was to rise on the twin backs of brawn and brains, without inheritance. It was utterly new – its roads, houses, industries. There had been nothing. Thousands of newcomers made it something.

Until the arrival, for instance, of large numbers of Irish labourers to build the huge dock, there had been no Catholic church here since the Reformation. Their arrival resulted in one and then two more.

Emigrant ships out of the Baltic, laden with persecuted Jews whose first landfall was to be Grimsby, were romanticised by the Victorians and given crews of jolly tars. In reality their harrowing journeys scarcely warranted the music which did not sweeten the pill.

There had been no synagogue but the arrival here, in hopeful transit from the Baltic, of considerable numbers of Jews fleeing the loathsome Russian pogroms, resulted in one. The Jewish immigration is fascinating and requires further exploration than that admirably started by Daphne and Leon Gerlis in

West Marsh paper mills, Grimsby, from the air.

1986 – *The Story of the Grimsby Jewish Community* (Humberside Leisure Services). These unhappy people would arrive in Grimsby bound, ideally, for America and would be introduced to this country – this town – by an immigration clerk who, frequently baffled by Russian surnames, would equip them with new, English, ones at a stroke of his pen. Thus did Mr Kaminski become Mr Kay, thus did Solomon Abelowitz become Solomon Bennett, glass merchant. And so on.

Many of Grimsby's Jewish hopefuls made the extended rail journey to Leeds, and no further. Many more made it all the way, via Liverpool, to America. One wonders, even now, whether the subsequently internationally famous made first landfall in Grimsby. Those who stayed here were the most impoverished and Grimsby magistrates had the unhappy chore of deciding, on a basis of ability to subsist, whether they stayed or were returned to a terrible fate in Russia's Baltic provinces. Those who made some arbitrary grade proved highly contributory. Grimsby's first Jewish mayor, Moses Abrahams, was appointed in 1900.

Because the old town was so small there had been no need of a public transport system. But the spread of streets and the development of hundreds of acres of farmland, marsh, fitties and carrs resulted in one. And then there came the schools, tens of them and the shops of every variety. There was suddenly a need for fire brigade and, naturally, a much expanding police force.

The rate of Grimsby's growth from 1860 to 1890, for instance, was enormous and expertise of a medical, scholastic, engineering and legal nature came here to advise and show the way in all things – from elaborate drainage systems to coping with the horrors of a smallpox epidemic.

In 1891 all this endeavour was crowned by the bestowal of County Borough status on the town and the creation of a knighthood for the then mayor, Henry Bennett, thus creating a local figurehead. Had a Grimsby man been knighted before? If so it had been centuries before.

By then people could look back with some satisfaction on their achievement.

In a short space of time Grimsby had exchanged

Alf Bannister (1868–1931), trawler baron, who rose from poverty to prosperity, and whose sporadic brushes with Royalty became legendary, thought he might have been in line for a knighthood, and said so. He was joking. But had he been knighted it would have warmed the hearts of Grimsby and the fishing trade, which had no greater advocate.

Henry Lewis Taylor (1860–1922) an impoverished lad who, famously, walked to Grimsby from Bristol, ultimately founding a trawling concern which survived to the end.

from being a boom town into a respectable and prosperous place.

A second generation was taking hold of the reins of industry and government, and no longer thought of themselves as Brixham or Suffolk or Yorkshire people. They were Grimsby people. The place – and they – had arrived and they formed a welcoming committee for thousands others yet to come and prosper in their wake. And come they did.

While dock building and timber and grain and coal and railways had formed Grimsby's first planks upon which fish was to build the remaining edifice,

it was to be jam making and paper making and brewing and engineering and food production that was yet, in 1891, to arrive and give that rounded feeling which comes with not having all your eggs in one, fishy, basket.

Moss, the Earl of Lonsdale's blacksmith, came to Grimsby in 1852 from Penrith, having heard that there were jobs going on the dock construction. But here in Grimsby he was no longer 'Moss' but William Moss, Mr Moss.

And when the dock was done he began his own smithing firm and went into smack fishing. Both his sons, Fred and Tom, became aldermen, both became mayors of the borough and both became very

Frank Barrett (1861–1941) seen here in his mayoral robes, was orphaned in India, came home, was a postman, came to Grimsby aged 17 and, two years later, became secretary to the Grimsby Smackowners' Association. In 1882 he joined a steam trawling company in a similar capacity and, in 1896, formed his own company, the Orient. His involvement with every aspect of the town's life was exemplary, and his generosity to it enduring. Frank Barrett's life encapsulates all that was best and contributory to Grimsby's rise and establishment.

Sir James Blindell (1884–1937) came to Grimsby aged 17 as a shoe shop assistant, opened his own shop 11 years later and eventually owned a chain of shops. A devout Liberal, he became MP for Boston in 1929 and thus began a brief but meteoric Parliamentary career culminating in his appointment as Junior Lord of the Treasury, the court dress of which office he wears in this study. He was greatly involved in Grimsby's civic and hospital life, but was killed when his motor car overturned near Stickford. Lady Blindell survived.

wealthy. Fred's wife was the only sister of MP George Doughty.

Alfred Cook, a local lad, began work at the age of nine in 1854 and became managing director of the Grimsby and North Sea Fishing Company. Alf Bannister, a railwayman's son, went to see as a cook on a smack and became a giant of the fishing industry. There are those yet who recall him at the wheel of his Rolls-Royce. Consider the penniless Harry Lewis Taylor, who walked to Grimsby from Bristol. He, too, eventually owned a fleet of trawlers. The army orphan, Frank Barrett, came here

Arthur Jeffs (1866–1945) was one of the nine children of George Jeffs who, with his brother Charles, came to Grimsby from Ramsgate to found one of the best known of the many trawling firms which succumbed to the post-World War One depression. Arthur Jeffs continued to run the firm's engineering business which long survived the trawling concern. The Jeffs were pioneers in many fields – one had the first electric car in the town – and were contributors to municipal and other aspects of town life.

penniless, prospered and was one of Grimsby's greatest benefactors having become a wealthy man.

This list is not endless but it could be considerable. Who does not know of the grandson of Shadrach Fitzherbert Nickerson, smack owner? Who has not heard of the son of Tom Ross, the 14-year-old Filey lad who worked for 10 years as a smack hand? And what of the 16-year-old Hitchin boy, Jim Blindell, the Grimsby shoe shop assistant who was to become knighted and a Junior Lord at the Treasury?

Remember, if you will, Edwin Bacon, the illiterate son of a rake of a father who fled unhappiness far away for a cabin boy's job on a Hamburg steamer out of Grimsby. And remember his rise to fame and fortune ...and that of William Butt, the Gloucestershire sawyer who sought a job in a Grimsby timber yard and founded one of the most enduring of all Grimsby's fishing concerns.

Remember them all.

The Lettens from Gravesend, the Jeffs whose pioneering patriarch fell off the pier at the fish docks while seeing his smacks off to sea ...and drowned.

When R.W. (Bob) Roberts, a poor boy from Barking, was 14, he was taken on by a smackowner called Thorpe and worked hard – and was made a partner. And when Thorpe died he inherited the business. Roberts (1857–1918) prospered and became wealthy... and an alderman and, in 1909, mayor. He never forgot the less fortunate, and Grimsby hospital benefited from his endless generosity. Grimsby espoused his type completely.

Samuel Everingham Green (on the right) with one of his sons, Neal (short for Cornelius). Green came to Grimsby aged 12 and found work as a hand on a smack. He was a director of one of the first steam fishing companies. Another of his sons became joint managing director of the Ross Group.

And there was young Robert Roberts, a poor lad from Barking when he came here in 1869 and who became mayor in 1910. Samuel Everingham Green was a 12-year-old smack hand from Hull. Yet against all odds he prospered. One of his sons was to live in the finest houses in the county.

Alec Black, a pastrycook's son, was to become a millionaire and one of the town's greatest philanthropists, while the story of the Sleights depends on the initial George, later raised to a baronetcy, who started life as a cockleboy on Cleethorpes beach and was to die leaving £1 million – and that in 1921.

All these stories of rags to riches – and there are

many more – were accomplished in Grimsby, a tolerant and welcoming town where all that mattered was a will to succeed and to become, in turn, part of the place, and a contributor to its success.

> Grimsby's a town by the Humber
> Noted for haddock and cod,
> Where the Smethursts speak only to Bennetts
> And the Bennetts speak only to God.

This pre-World War One ditty, in which the surnames are variable according to the company you kept, summed up the new establishment which had finally gelled from the host of people who had converged on the town. There were no blue-blooded

From what is described as a modest background – his mother sold cakes – came one of Grimsby's greatest figures, the trawling magnate, horse-racing enthusiast and great philanthropist Alec Black who, via schoolmastering, went on to the docks and eventually owned the largest fleet of trawlers in the world. Sir Alec (1873–1942) won a reputation for both carefully thought-out and spontaneous magnanimity. The memory of him lives on and his enthusiasm for the frozen food industry is, even today, contributory to the town's success.

aristocrats here to assume the head of the table, no squires, no bishops, no literary giants or retired generals, none to challenge the worthy but rather unworldly self-made pontoon peers.

Grimsby's hierarchy was, from the start, based on commercial success. But its social structure was to come from a curious source. Sir George Doughty's first wife died in 1904. Three years later and while on a Parliamentary visit to India, the 53-year-old MP met, on a liner, a very beautiful 28-year-old Australian journalist, Eugenia Stone who, to the delighted surprise of Grimsby, he married.

The new Lady Doughty was an eye-opener for the town, a sophisticated worldly professional who immediately transformed Sir George's gloomy household into a centre of social life. She was embraced by church and chapel – despite being a Roman Catholic – and threw herself wholeheartedly into the life of the town, a more than superb consort for her husband, then the uncrowned King of Grimsby. She wrote in the town's daily paper – the *Telegraph* (which her husband owned) – and she encouraged the town's ladies to be more than wives and mothers, and to take a part in its life.

But it was to be Lady Doughty's protegé, a bank manager's daughter, who was to add enduring substance to the town's structure. Dorothy Clapham was the only daughter of George Clapham, the manager of Smith Ellison's bank at Riby Square. His shrewd judgement had determined the future of so many of Grimsby's aspiring businessmen, particularly those concerned with the fishing industry. No man knew the new trawler owners better and to no other man were the trawler owners so grateful – even beholden.

The Claphams, great friends of the Doughtys, were leading Tories, yet without 'side', observers, all-embracing. And when, towards the end of World War One, the by-then-widowed Lady Doughty left Grimsby, never to return, she handed over her literary and social mantle to the girl she had been encouraging for years, the dutiful and clever Dorothy Clapham. Miss Clapham – she never married

– allied her bank manager father's discretion as a keeper of confidences to an acute sense of purpose, combining them in the weekly column in the paper in which she had inherited a role. It was known as Lavender's Column and in it, week after week, year after year, appeared the apparently inconsequential notes of what appeared to be a purely social nature. In fact Dorothy Clapham was creating a social framework in which people came to feel a sense of belonging. Never was a column so well read and, over a period of 40 years, many felt that inclusion in it provided establishment.

But it was through it, and because of her drive and enthusiasm, that Miss Clapham created most of the local women's organisations, leagues and associations, many of which endure. Dorothy Clapham was perhaps the single most effective creator of the town's hierarchy. She was a very serious and single-minded pioneer who died, in harness, in 1969.

But by 1969 the town was changing rapidly.

George Lowe Alward (1842–1933) was a Rechabite, a teetotaller. He was a secularist – an atheist, a free-thinker. He was an author, a magistrate, a Fellow of the Royal Society of Arts and he built the most exceptional house Humberston ever saw. He was also, so they say, a bore. But he built the first steam trawlers out of Grimsby and, for a period in his life, showed the way for all to follow.

Charles Frederick Carter (1843–1922), seen here seated, was born at Rochford, Essex 'of humble parents', came to Grimsby via Bath, Banbury, Hull, Louth, Gainsborough and Huddersfield, arriving in 1868 aged 25 and opening a draper's shop in Freeman Street. Five years later his talents were harnessed by the directors of the Coal, Salt and Tanning company as their company secretary and he built the firm into an international concern. His brother, Arthur John Carter (1847–1918) became a power-in-the-land in a burgeoning Australia. His son, Walter Carter, opened the Royal Insurance Company's first office in Grimsby and his grandson was Sir Walker Kelly Carter (his other grandfather being the trawler owner Henry Kelly). Sir Walker (1900–1985), educated at Repton and Sidney Sussex, was for many years chairman of the Lindsey Quarter Sessions. With C.F. Carter in this picture is his lifelong friend Sir George Moody (1860–1939), knighted in 1926. In partnership with Henry Kelly and much assisted by the money of George Brown, the second-generation Grimsby builder, they founded the once well-known firm which bore their names, and the Crown Steam Fishing Company in 1902. They once sent one of their trawlers, the *Lyric*, to the West African coast to explore trawling possibilities... and to dredge for pearl oysters.

Trawler and smack owners, fish merchants and allied fish dock trades

Allen, trawlers	Brixham
Alward, trawler and smack owners	Brixham
Bacon, trawler owners	Brightlingsea
Bannister, trawler owners	Native (Cleethorpes)
Barrett, trawler owner etc	Plumstead, Essex (born India)
Baskcomb, trawler owners	Barking (orig. Woolwich and Eltham)
Baxter, smacks	Greenwich and Brixham
Black, trawler owner	Native (Grimsby)
Butt, trawler owners etc	Minchinghampton, Glos
Campbell, smack owner & builder	Native (Grimsby)
Carter, coal salt	Rochford, Essex
Chapman, trawler owners, merchant	Native (Cleethorpes)
Charlton, shipwright, engineer	Stockholm
Cleve, merchants	Native (Grimsby)
Cook (Markham), trawler owner	Tendring, Essex
Crampin, trawler owners	Native (Cleethorpes)
Croft Baker, trawler owners etc	King's Lynn, Norfolk
Dobson, trawler owners	Native (Grimsby)
Doughty, trawler owners etc	Wideoken, Northumberland
Forge, smack owner	Barking
Franklin, trawler owners	Native, Grimsby
Gidley, smacks	Ramsgate
Goodwin, trawler owner	Hull
Grant, trawler owners	Native
Green, owners and curers etc	Hull
Guzzwell, smack and trawler owners	Brixham
Hill, trawler owner	Barking
Hopwood, trawlers	Yorkshire
Jeffs G, trawler owners, engineers	Ramsgate, Kent
Jeffs C, ditto	Margate
Kelly, trawler owners	Lincoln and native
Kennedy, smack owner	Barking
Knott, merchants	Ramsgate
Lambert, trawler owner	Hull
Letten, trawler owners	Gravesend
Little, merchants and owners	Hull
Mackrill, trawler owner	Mablethorpe
Marsden, fishing	Huddersfield
Melhuish, merchant	Barking

Meadows, smack owner	Hastings
Moody, trawler owner	Louth Marsh
Morris, trawler owner	Hull
Moss, trawler owners	Penrith
Mudd, smack owners, merchants	Holbrook, Suffolk
Nickerson, smacks	Gravesend
Osborne, trawler owner	Native (Cleethorpes)
Roberts, trawler owners	Barking
Robinson, trawler owners	Native (Cleethorpes)
Ross, trawler owners and merchants	Filey
Rushworth, smacks, trawler owners	London
Sleight, trawler owners, merchants	Native (Old Clee)
Smethurst, smack and trawler owners	Newark
Suggitt, smack	Easington
Taylor, trawler owners	Bristol
Watkinson, merchants	Market Rasen

Commercial and retail trades. Not fish docks

Abrahams, pawnbroker etc	Posen, Prussia, via Hull
Bannister, Edward, coal	Hull
Bellamy, mineral waters etc	Horncastle, via Louth. (ex publicans)
Bennett, timber	Native (Grimsby)
Blindell, shoeshops (later MP)	Hitchin, Herts
Bradley, (Orby) coal merchants	South Cockerington
Brown, builders	Irby-on-Humber
Carlbom, shipping	Sweden
Chambers, grocers	Sheffield
Clapham, banker	Louth
Cook, (Markham) chemist	Hull
Crosby, brewer	Nottingham
Curry, theatre owner	Hull
Dixon, paper maker	Oughtibridge, Sheffield
Doig, shipbuilders	Dundee
Eason, travel agent etc	Moulton, Spalding
Ellis, timber	Newark
Evison, licensed trade	Lincolnshire
Falconer, coopers	Scotland
Forge, smacks, licensed trade	Barking
Gait, printer	Brighton
Goddard, builder	Snaith, Yorkshire
Goodhand, builder	North Somercotes

Kay (Kaminski), jeweller	Birmingham
Gee, store owner, banker	Redruth
Harrison, stockbroker	Hull
Irish, millers	Tadcaster
Lee, furnishers	Leeds
Draper, scrap metal	Hull
Smith (Guy), store owner	Hainton, Lincs
Stockil, ironmonger	Northallerton
Nidd, jeweller	Clipsham, Rutland
Hewins, builder	North Thoresby
Hewitt, brewers	Doncaster
Hewitt, jewellers	Ulceby, N Lincs
Hewson, timber	Native
Hill, mineral waters	Native (Grimsby)
Johnson, chemist	Utterby
Josse, coal exporter (later MP)	Caen, France
Loft, veterinary etc	Native (Healing)
Riggall, grocer	Gayton-le-Wold
Maddison, baker	Boston
Marshall, millers	Native (Grimsby)
Noble, confectioners	Hunmanby, Yorks
Oldroyd, stores	Yorkshire
Osmond, cattle foods etc	Spalding
Overbeck, brewer etc	Germany
Pettifer, builder	Yorkshire
Smith (George), chemist	Berwick-upon-Tweed
Southworth, grocer	Chorley, Lancs
Store, accountant	Louth
Sutcliffe, shipping agents	West Hartlepool
Tate, grocer	Garton, Holderness
Tickler, jam maker (later MP)	Withern, Alford
Tierney, tobacconist	Ireland
Towle, builder	Caistor
Womersley, stores (later MP)	Bradford (via Hull)
Would, builder (via trawling)	Belchford

Professionals: doctors, etc

Anningson, Dr	Burnley
Barker, solicitor	York
Bates, (Anderson) solicitor	Native (Grimsby)
Birtles, police	Oldham
Bloomer, solicitor	Worcestershire
Brown, (Waudby) solicitor	Hull
Butler, police	Barnsley
Chapman, solicitor	Native (Cleethorpes)
Daubney solicitor	Native (Grimsby)
Dawber-Enderby, Dr	Boston
Farebrother, architect	Corby, Lincs (Londoner)
Fisher, Dr	Native (Cleethorpes)
Grange, solicitor	Native (Grimsby)
Haddelsey, solicitor	Caistor
Heeler, town clerk	Birmingham
Keay, dentist	Alyth, Perthshire
Keetley, Dr	Native (Grimsby)
Leppington, Dr	Market Rasen
Mason, solicitor	Keddington, Louth
Markham, Canon A.A.	Saxby All Saints
Mountain, solicitor	Braceborough, Stamford
Scaping, arch	Hull (Irish)
Spring, Dr	Boston, USA (Irish)
Stephenson, Dr	Native (Grimsby)
Stirling, police	Aberdeen
Wallace, Dr	Berwick
Wilkin, solicitor etc	Native (Grimsby)
Wintringham, solicitor	Native (Grimsby)

KINGS

THE death on 8 June 1913 of William Grange, Grimsby's Bismarck, was a shock despite the fact that he was within a month of his 92nd birthday. He had been at the core of the town since the reign of William IV. Thus 70 years of knowledge and of recollection, for Grange remained alert to the end, were denied. He had meant to write his memoirs but never had the time.

His firm, Grange and Wintringham had lost a founding father and its partners knew that the sway of The Offfice – as his premises were widely known – were over. The town wondered what life would be like without him. Most of all, the Town Council, which had relied so heavily on his guidance, wondered how it might manage. There was a magic in the very surname. And, fortunately, there was a Grange ready, however reluctantly, to step into his father's shoes. And he actually looked like Bismarck.

Dr Ernest Leigh Grange, now 53, had been his father's understudy as town clerk for 14 years. He was no stranger to the intricacies of council meetings and had all the concomitant tact to cope with its

Lt Colonel Dr Ernest Leigh Grange, the reluctant town clerk.

members. Without alternative, the council approached him. Dr Grange, in turn, knew where his duty lay. He was the recently retired (1910) commanding officer of the Grimsby artillery unit. He was a product of the Ley's School, and Emmanuel College, Cambridge, a solicitor, the nominated deputy town clerk, clerk to the local magistrates and a one-time editor of *Lincolnshire Notes and Queries*. Above all he was his father's son.

He replied to the council's desperate request. 'I shall do all I can to assist you until you have appointed a new town clerk. I shall not be a candidate for that position. It is my desire to be released from my official duties as soon as you can, convenient with the business of the Corporation.' Grasping at the offer, the council accepted his terms.

Happily for Dr Grange, his tenure of office lasted for only a year. In 1914 John William Jackson was appointed town clerk. He was, incredibly in view of Grimsby's current status and population – 75,000 – the first full-time town clerk the town had ever had. The Granges had been 'incidental'. With Jackson's appointment so passed the close municipal involvement of The Office

The old and the new. Led by the newly appointed chief constable, Charles Butler and followed by the mayor's sergeant Mr C.E. Dennis in his archaic full fig, comes the town clerk, John William Jackson, taking part in his final mayoral parade along Victoria Street in 1937 before retirement. With them is the new mayor, Councillor Charles Edwin Franklin who was an engine driver.

Sir George Doughty seen here (in top hat, left) on Empire Day 1912 was the parvenu of whom his snobbish fellow MPs in the Commons disapproved. But Grimsby didn't.

L.W. Heeler (extreme left), town clerk from 1938 to 1958.

and Grange and Wintringham became, mercifully perhaps, a firm of family solicitors, a burden shed.

Jackson came to Grimsby from Salford and brought a new independent professionalism to the Borough. A bachelor, his subsequent involvement in World War One brought him an OBE. He was a safe pair of hands for so burgeoning a town and his involvement from his home in Park Drive was total. His retirement in 1938 brought a very different type of man to Grimsby's tiller.

Leslie William Heeler, the Birmingham-born deputy town clerk of Stockport was 33 when he came to Grimsby, a brilliant, aesthetic, lean and highly capable man, learned in the law, lacking in tact. He was an autocrat, ill-suited to the rigmarole of democracy, impatient with the meanderings of local councillors of all levels of intelligence. They regretted appointing him and, in 1939, he was sacked. But then war broke out and his notice was rescinded.

Heeler's great contribution to the town involved the post-war development of the Humber Bank and the divergence of industry when fishing began, trans-

parently, to wane in importance. Heeler did not keep a low profile and a celebrated post-war court case involving a house he rented did nothing to embellish his office. In 1958, and after a long succession of stormy council meetings, Heeler was sacked for the second time, departing tearfully for Kettering and a solicitor's practice...and a subsequent retirement in Dorchester where he died, aged 91, in 1996.

His successor was the altogether more tactful F.W. Ward, who was to pilot the town through declining years, an agreeable man with complete respect for the views of the councillors to whom he was bound to dispense legalese.

Another helm was provided by the town's MP. Only months after the death of William Grange, George Doughty died. Doughty was born and bred locally – and proud of it – had made a fortune as a builder, dragging himself up by the bootstrings in true Victorian fashion and, in his 30s, retired. His wealth had been harnessed by go-ahead smack owners and he had made a second fortune out of steam trawling. His sweeping into parliamentary victory over the county establishment was the stuff

The *Eastern Daily Telegraph* (later the *Evening Telegraph*) which George Doughty's money established and which was designed to be his mouthpiece in the town, is seen here in March 1898, the first anniversary of its foundation.

of dreams and, with a 1910 hiccup when Tom Wing became, for 10 months, the town's MP, George Doughty held the reins.

Newspaper proprietor – the *Grimsby Telegraph* – and supremely self-confident, he was the very epitome of Grimsby, shrugging off the critical views of Westminster – which regarded him as a parvenu – and doing all in his power to promote his town and its staple industry. His death in 1914, so soon after that of Grange, and in the gloom cast by the gathering clouds of war, prompted that other captain of local industry, Thomas George Tickler, to stand for the Tory seat – and win.

Tickler had also, as the newspapers had it, 'risen from the ranks'. He was 66 and had amassed a fortune making and selling jam. Born at Withern near Louth, a miller's son, he had begun Grimsby's diversification from fish and timber by establishing a jam factory in the town, much aided by a substantial War Office order for jam for Boer War troops. This fortune was to be consolidated during World War One for the same reasons.

Tickler too felt he was a son of Grimsby and, in 1919, his wartime duty done, stood down to make way for Tom Sutcliffe. Sutcliffe was a second generation man, his surname a household word in the town. His father, John, an MS & L man through and through, had established a thriving shipping business. His brother, Jack had been one of the town's most memorable mayors, and his nephew, Albert, had the famous private zoo off Bargate. But Tom Sutcliffe, Haileybury and Oxford behind him, had left town to live in Stallingborough and to hunt with the Brocklesby. He found parliamentary work tiring (if not tiresome) and stood down in 1922.

Walter Womersley now topped the polls and became Grimsby's last Tory – and last local – MP. Womersley, who had begun work at the age of 10 in a Bradford factory, had become a shop manager at 18 and, at 21, had a haberdashery of his own. So proud of his achievement was he that he included it all in his entry in *Who's Who*. But after serving in Churchill's cabinet throughout the war and being

When you're in a jam, here I am. T.G. Tickler MP in the wake of Sir George Doughty, jam maker, employer of thousands, whose plum and apple jam became a mainstay of the British Army in World War One. The empty tins were converted to extemporary hand grenades and became known as Tickler's Artillery.

raised to the baronetcy, his popularity and majority stood for nothing in the Labour landslide election of 1945 and Grimsby returned Major Kenneth Younger. He was the first of a trio of Labour Members, the second Anthony Crosland who famously became Foreign Secretary and, following his untimely death in 1977, Austin Mitchell who currently represents the town with an independence and individuality refreshing in modern politics.

That other principal figure in Grimsby's, and any town's, past was the chief constable. Despite all the ingredients for crime, Grimsby was not a notably lawless town...which was probably just as well for the small police force was, in its early years, not efficient. But after the 20-year tenure of office by

Tom Sutcliffe, Tickler's Tory successor, an urbane bachelor, a country gentleman whose interest in hunting (with the Brocklesby) was greater than for politics. He died as a result of being thrown by his horse.

John Ross Campbell, Job Waldram took over in 1879 and with only 31 constables – a figure rising to 51 by the time he retired in 1891 – laid the foundations for a good force.

Henry Pickersgill (1848–1925), whose private behaviour left much to be desired, succeeded him and resigned rather than be dismissed in 1899. John Fisher, who had learned all he knew of policing in Liverpool was then appointed, but died within two years. Thus did John Stirling (1864–1938) come here. Stirling was to head the force for 30 years, a big and handsome man, capable and strict, 6ft 3in yet the shortest of seven sons.

His deputy, Charles Tartellin succeeded him in

1930 and, following his death in office in 1934, Frank Bunn held the post for two years until Charles Butler's appointment in 1936.

The adhesive between these several 1930s comings and goings was Supt Arthur Birtles OBE, twice acting chief constable but never appointed. And when, in 1938, he finally retired after 40 years in police uniform, he was promptly recalled at the outbreak of war to serve as Butler's deputy until 1946. An Oldham man, Birtles died in 1963 aged 86. He was easily the longest served member of the Borough force and had founded the athletic society on which Butler was to build mightily.

Charles Butler was a remarkable man. Grimsby was to be very fortunate. Born in Barnsley in 1893 where his father, George Butler was chief constable, there was only one life for him. At 17 he was a constable, at 21 a sergeant... this in Rotherham where, in 1914, and at an incredibly young age he recruited and controlled the town's howitzer brigade and heavy artillery battery and reorganised and commanded the town's special constabulary. In 1916, aged 23 he was promoted to inspector and became an officer in the Royal Flying Corps. At 29 he was chief constable of Maidstone and, full of experience, and bemedalled, came to Grimsby in 1936. He was 43. The Borough force was 100 strong.

Butler's passion for sporting endeavour, particularly cricket and, overwhelmingly, football led to the establishment of the most efficient, most loyal and happy force Grimsby has ever known. Its football team won the English Police Federation Cup annually and played against semi-professional clubs in Lincolnshire League football. The team was, in major part, composed of ex-professionals recruited to the force by Butler. He insisted, with a smile, that they were policemen first and foremost. He guided the town, with Birtles at his side, through World War Two and retired in 1962 aged 69. His successor was Grimsby's last chief constable, John Angus, Gateshead-born, who died in 1974.

In English mayoral processions a cleric in office is often to be seen. He is generally an Anglican priest

Sir Walter Womersley Bt (seated centre), one-time Postmaster General and Minister of Pensions, was Grimsby's last Tory MP.

and he represents the community spiritual. The formative years of Grimsby's launch into the firmament of fame were dominated by one such clergyman. The Revd – later Canon – Robert Ainslie (1811–1895) was promoted to Grimsby in 1856 by his cousin at Hainton, Edward Heneage. St James' was then in the gift of the Heneages. The heir to a baronetcy (which he chose not to accept), half-Spanish – his father had married his mother while soldiering with Wellington in the Peninsular – and extremely wealthy, he found a church in total decline, unattended and ruinous.

His predecessor, who lived in London, had condescended to visit Grimsby for one month a year – and that for many years. Ainslie, an austere, academic bachelor did not court popularity. Nor did

he win it. Respect was his, even fear. For Ainslie was a man who saw what had to be done and had the private wherewithal and the Heneage brief to do it – and without reference. Arriving at the age of 46, he stayed 23 years, during which time he totally restored the derelict church and created, and had built, seven schools, paying for six of them entirely.

By no means all of Grimsby's newcomers were of Low Church persuasion; Ainslie was a High Church man with leanings towards Roman Catholicism, probably a result of his mother's past and the recusant Heneages. None did as much for his parish as did Ainslie for Grimsby. He was to be, post mortem, utterly ignored, even wilfully erased. Bob Lincoln did not mention him. Gillett, disgracefully, does not mention him. Shaw mentions him once and

Major The Hon Kenneth Younger (later Sir Kenneth), Grimsby's first Labour MP.

Anthony Crosland, Foreign Secretary, who died in office in February 1977.

The splendid uniformed figure of Chief Constable John Stirling. On the left is Alderman Isidore Abrahams and, after Stirling, are HM Inspector of Constabulary, Sir W.L. Atcherley, Alderman R.G. Kitching, the town clerk J.W. Jackson and, right, Supt Tartellin, chief constable in waiting.

named after Edward Heneage's wife) he brought seemliness, sobriety and the faith to a raucous and vulgar new parish.

In so doing, he won a respect from the employed fishermen whose occasional high-handed treatment brought them into desperate contact with the law. This intimate, unique contact and experience resulted in Meddings' role as a go-between in industrial quarrels and a recognition by the courts. Meddings was both chaplain to the local militia and the official local Admiralty chaplain. After 20 years in his lively billet, he left and died in Tunbridge Wells in 1922. A wealthy man, he had one son, Eustace, who, as a small boy, laid the foundation stone of Strand Street Girls' School in 1897. Eustace later went to Eton, the first Grimsby boy so to do.

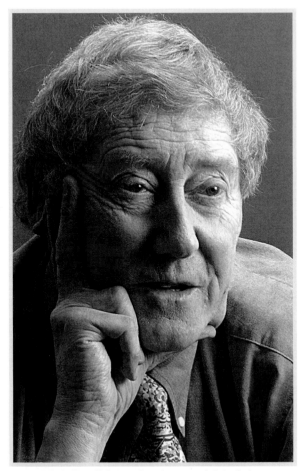

Austin Mitchell, well-known broadcaster and Grimsby's current long-serving MP.

spells his name incorrectly. Anderson Bates says nothing of him. The truth is that Ainslie was the new broom. They are seldom hailed. He died aged 84 and is buried in Chingford where his father had once been MP.

The town's second important Anglican padre was Richard Meddings (1854–1922), the most memorable vicar of St Andrew's, the site for which, in Freeman Street, had been bought by Ainslie in 1859. Meddings arrived in 1889 and while Ainslie had coped with Top Town, Meddings had the often unenviable task of catering to parishioners of a much rougher nature, his parish dominated by the docks and the public house. From his colossal vicarage in Eleanor Street (the thoroughfare is

Charles Tartellin (1879–1934) chief constable of Grimsby.

Twice the bridesmaid, never the bride. Supt Arthur Birtles, twice acting chief constable.

...St James' Church as he found it...

Canon Robert Ainslie...

...and his memorial, the interior of St James' in 1908.

The Revd Richard Meddings, an
Anglican in Freeman Street...

...and St Andrew's Church where
he dispensed not only the gospel
but secular wisdom.

REVELATIONS

THE entitlement to bear military rank has always assisted in the formation of a hierarchy which permeates civilian life. So it was to be in Grimsby. The first unit to be raised in the town, to counter the perceived threat from Napoleon, was the Great Grimsby Volunteer Infantry, raised in 1803, the town clerk, George Babb, commanding. It existed for 10 years. Its initial members – there were about 60 of them – included the surnames Lister, Lusby, Marshall, Chapman, Bates, Joys, Sinderson, Bellamy, Robinson, Hollingsworth, West, Appleyard and so on. Armed with pikes, a few muskets and swords, they combined with the North Lincoln Legion, a body of cavalry raised by Lord Yarborough, to keep an eye on the dunes.

During this period, Lincolnshire, like all eastern districts, was almost a county in arms, the Lord Lieutenant having been told to raise local units. Lincolnshire not only had many parish infantry units but at least 11 yeomanry troops. In addition units from other counties, like the Somerset Fencible

Lt Colonel Alderman James Reed, mayor of Grimsby, Portmaster, the MS & L man who, in 1864, lost his mother, his wife and his only son in the space of one month. He died in 1892, with a very full life behind him.

Cavalry – and the 3rd Dragoons from the Regular Army – were sent as supplements. The Grimsby infanteers had their own Colour which, in 1813, was placed in St James's Church, by tradition and for safe keeping. However, when the restoration of the church took place under Canon Ainslie many years later, it passed into private hands and, in 1874, was acquired by Colonel James Reed. On his death, his son, the solicitor Alfred J. Reed, kept it at his home in Welholme Road. But in 1925, and having lived in London for some time, Reed returned the relic to the town and the then mayor, Alderman Frank Barrett had it replaced in St James's.

For more than 40 subsequent years Grimsby (and England) had little need for volunteers, a calm ruffled in 1859 because of a less specific threat from Napoleon III which resulted in the raising of fresh volunteers. The Commander-in-Chief, the Duke of

Sgt Major Thomas Webster Smith (1822–1906), ex-3rd Light Dragoons, mentor to the Lincolnshire Light Horse.

president. When he retired as portmaster in 1884, retaining all his ranks and titles, a piece of music called *Outward Bound* was commissioned in his honour and the front cover of that forms part of the jacket of this book.

The messes of both regiments were stiffened by Bennetts and Wintringhams and Granges from The Office and the town's two principal Anglican padres became chaplains.

In 1860, the Earl of Yarborough raised, as heir to the Legion, the First Lincolnshire Light Horse, the Earl of Yarborough's Own, a small squadron-strength unit, also with a band, and largely composed of the Earl's chums and relatives and tenants. It was trained by Sgt Major Thomas Webster (1822–1906), who lived in Burgess Street and had served 25 years with the 3rd Light Dragoons, fighting at Moodkee, Sobraon and through the Indian Mutiny. The Light Horse was fortunate in him.

Cambridge, worried about defence and visited the east coast. 'I think the mouth of Humber is a point which cannot be overlooked as a great emporium of our trade.' Grimsby mattered!

Both Daubney and Grange, showing the way, joined up, and the railway company built the artillery barracks in Victoria Street. Grimsby soon sported both an infantry and an artillery unit. Each had a band, useful adjuncts to civic pride and, with a little assistance from what few retired regular soldiers were about, became efficient. The gunners were soon commanded by that man of many parts, Lt Colonel James Reed, friend of Sir Edward Watkin, from 1860 the MS & L Portmaster, alderman, magistrate, mayor (in 1872), governor of Clee Grammar School and the Conservative Club's vice

The redoubtable Countess of Yarborough, CO of the Light Horse.

Major Rowland Sleight.

The South African War of 1899–1902 did not result in either of Grimsby's militia units setting off to war, although a number of individuals did enlist in the Lincolnshire Regiment, volunteers all, and were hailed on their safe homecoming as heroes, feted and rewarded with engraved watches.

One of those famously to go to war was the young Roland Sleight (1877–1947), perhaps the first of the sons of Grimsby trawler owners to go to public school (Rugby), who joined the Queensland Mounted Infantry. He was a subsequent instigator of the Lincolnshire Yeomanry and he and his brother Ernest (later Sir Ernest), an infantryman, were to propound volunteer service to the end of their days.

Roland Sleight, incidentally, was one of the three officers of the post-Boer War Yeomanry to be able to afford the lavish Lancer-style full dress uniform of that regiment – the others being the Earls of Ancaster and Yarborough.

The military offered an alternative to the town council to become involved in local affairs and afforded the benefits of a splendid uniform and the entitlement to rank. This was all very important in late 19th century Grimsby where newcomers sought bonds of friendship and comradeship and sources aside from public house or chapel, and aside from Freemasonry – which thrived in the town. The military brought together men from all classes and all professions and trades and was 'pure'.

The Royal Navy had not courted Grimsby – despite an earlier recommendation to do so and

another, spurned by the authorities, to use the port during the Crimean War. Thus the military allowed people to partake of 'tradition' of which Grimsby had little of any kind.

The outbreak of war in 1914 should have been no surprise to Grimsby. Indeed the vision of invasion had once again been appreciated. The mayor, J.W. Eason issued a warning to the population:

'It is extremely improbable that Grimsby will be attacked either from sea, land or air. But should the unexpected happen...

'A warning will be given by buzzers, sounding continually for five minutes. Citizens are requested to behave in a way worthy of belonging to a great and brave nation.

'Keep out of the streets and remain in your groundfloor rooms. Extinguish all lights. Promptly obey any orders given by the military or the police.

'All exits from the town will be barred. I rely on the loyal and hearty co-operation of every citizen to preserve order and avoid panic.'

Grimsby did indeed behave in a worthy way – none more so than Councillor Eason's only son, Raymond, subaltern in the Chums, killed within seconds of the opening of the Battle of the Somme in 1916.

Ever since Erskine Childers' sensational novel *The Riddle of the Sands* was published in 1903, posturing a German invasion of the east coast, great attention had been paid to the town by very senior figures indeed. In 1907 Admiral Lord Charles Beresford brought the entire Channel Fleet here and had earnest conversation with local trawler owners concerning the appropriation of their ships for

Lord Yarborough in the full dress of the Lincolnshire Yeomanry.

Colonel John Tonge CMG (1864–1917) solicitor, CO of the Grimsby gunners, who died after being wounded in action.

minesweeping duties should war break out. Particularly prominent in these discussions was George Lowe Alward one of Grimsby's fishing pioneers who had already loaned two of his trawlers for experimental 'sweeping' off Portland. They had been conspicuously successful.

In 1909, by which time the rattle of German sabres could be heard distinctly, General Sir John French (the man who would lead the BEF in 1914) came to the town, ostensibly to meet Colonel Grange and to see the 5th Lincolns' new drill hall opened in Doughty Road in 1903. Two months after his visit, the gunners were issued with new 15 pounders, 'magnificent weapons' enthused the local press.

Grimsby and the Humber and especially the in-

creation deep water dock at Immingham were being taken very seriously, increasing numbers of visits by submarines (the first in 1907) reinforcing the point.

At the outbreak of war, the 5th Lincolns (TA) and the artillerymen were at full strength when mustered. The latter, commanded by solicitor Colonel John Tonge, son of the licensees of the Royal Hotel and then aged 49, were the first Territorial gunners to fire a shot in the war. Colonel Tonge died after being wounded in 1917, his unit taken over by Lt Colonel John Henry Hinton, his Riby Square practice by Mr Walter West.

In France the gunners were the recipients of considerable largesse from Grimsby and all supplied by Sir Alec Black, providing comforts from home. The 5th Lincolns, 24 officers and 780 other ranks strong – had the immediate task of providing guards for the wireless station at New Waltham and placing the docks in a state of defence. Battalion HQ was set up on the railway company steamer Dewsbury in the Royal Dock. But their place was taken by drafts from the Manchester Regiment and the 5th sailed for France. And with them went Major Ernest Sleight and Captain Oscar Dixon of the paper milling family.

Of the other two military units formed in Grimsby one, the Volunteer Training Corps is least recalled. It was raised, organised and financed by Lt Colonel Harry J.F. Crosby, manager of Hewitt's Brewery and managing director of the Palace Theatre. It was a training unit providing reinforcements for the Regular Army, but its members also guarded munition factories – there was one in Victoria Street – and 160 of its members manned searchlights on the Humber's banks. The VTC was disbanded in 1919. Poor Crosby shot himself in 1922.

Of the other military unit much has been – and continues to be – written. So great was the torrent of young men wishing to join the Colours in August 1914 that, across Britain, infantry battalions were formed from friends and associates and named Pals Battalions. In Grimsby these youthful volunteers, civilians all, were deemed Chums. And the name stuck. Patronised by the old squirearchy, commanded

The Grimsby gunners (Colonel Tonge centre) before embarkation for France.

The officers of the 5th Bn The Lincolns in October 1914. Back row, second left Lt Oscar Dixon, 5th left Lt R.D. Crosby. Third row, seated, second left, Captain Ernest Sleight. Front row, cross-legged 2nd Lt Harold Mountain (1879–1946) later Lt Colonel RA, Grimsby Borough Coroner from 1928 and Civil Defence controller in Grimsby in 1939.

Ernest Farebrother's artillery barracks in Victoria Street, commissioned by the MS & L and paid for by John Chapman MP is the backdrop to this delightful photograph of a 16-pounder gun team in 1905. On the lead horses are (nearest the camera) Battery Sgt Maj Tom W. Gill with Bdr Gus Appleyard who died in 1912. On the wheel horse is ex-regular gunner Dvr Harry Butty. Standing is Sgt Jim Cave. On the limber (with moustache) is Gnr Tom Berry and an unidentified man. But the outrider is the battery trumpeter Harry Appleyard, then aged 13, the son of Gus Appleyard, of Rathgar, Deansgrove, Grimsby who joined up aged 9½.

Trench photographs from World War One are few and far between. Therefore, reminders of those men who fought in the Grimsby Chums' Battalion are necessarily confined to studio portraits or pictures of their homespun training exercises at Brocklesby. Sufficient then this off-duty moment in the winter of 1914–15 with, from the left, CQMS Toby Atkinson, Captain Tom Baker, Captain W.S. Pratte, 2nd Lt Raymond Eason, 2nd Lt R. Coote Green. Raymond Eason was killed within seconds of the opening of the Battle of the Somme on 1 July 1916. Tom Baker was killed some minutes later. The toll was considerable.

by The Hon George Heneage of Hainton and given a billet by the Earl of Yarborough at Brocklesby, they were, perhaps, the true heirs to the old Great Grimsby Volunteer Infantry of Napoleonic times. But the fate of the 10th Battalion, the Lincolnshire Regiment, – the Grimsby Chums – was to be very different, and their sacrifice on the Somme and at Arras is well known. It is a fact that even today, almost a century and another world war away, their endeavours are still recalled and their memory revered.

But it was attack from the sea which focused military minds in 1914, a fear reinforced by hit-and-run raids by German warships on Scarborough and Hartlepool. The estuary forts – Bull and Haile Sands – were in the throes of building and two guns destined for the latter were set up at New Clee and a nine-pounder breech-loader was fixed to a railway wagon and ran up and down the Grimsby to Cleethorpes railway line searching for a target. Most of Grimsby's trawlers were commandeered as minesweepers (as planned) and served off the British Isles generally, in the Mediterranean and at Gallipoli. Altogether 305 of them were lost to enemy action during the course of the war and Grimsby's naval and RNR casualties totalled 375. The owners of these trawlers were given some compensation by the Admiralty, both for their use and when they were lost, mostly as victims of U-boats or mines and, occasionally, as in the case of the first to be sunk, the *Tubal Cain*, by gunfire.

The only air raids over the district were by Zeppelins and although bombs were dropped as near as Cleethorpes and Scartho, Grimsby itself did not suffer.

Grimsby's several newspapers had, by 1914, polarised into two which relayed censored reports of distant battles in most of which Grimsby's sons were involved.

This public participation was a desperate mix of gloom and rejoicing – the first because casualty lists were not censored and were published relentlessly. Nonetheless they were to prove a bond. We were all

in it now and we were all Grimbarians. The good news alleviated the sadness and when gallantry awards were made public, and when Grimsby people read of (for instance) Military Crosses being awarded to people called (for instance) Reggie Crosby, Frank Letten, Harry Falconer, Charles Emerson, Henry Chapman, John Wintringham, Edwin Nickerson, Bill Tickler, John Kennington and so on, they felt a reflected honour. Such awards, the public felt, did not merely belong to the recipients but to Grimbarians... and not to people from Gravesend or Peterhead. The pride was not that only of the families involved, but of the town as a whole.

And when it was all over, they returned to put behind them unspeakable horrors. Few had ever been beyond the town's boundaries in 1914. Most had never been abroad and almost none had ever taken part in any endeavour save of a domestic nature. The Great War of 1914–18 opened many eyes to affairs well beyond Grimsby.

Between the wars Grimsby's enthusiasm for not only the Territorial Army and the RNVR but also the new Air Training Corps was maintained. The Yeomanry, however, was, after distinguished service in Palestine, disbanded. A suggestion that they became an artillery unit was politely declined. The now obsolete gunners' barracks in Victoria Street was sold to the Graphite Oils Company and became a laboratory. That subsequently became Albert Gait's print works. New barracks were built in both Augusta Street and Westward Ho and the aerodrome at Waltham – later to be RAF Grimsby – became headquarters for an aero club which certainly introduced many Grimsby people to the joys and the hazards of flying, whetting many appetites for service in the RAF.

The 5th Lincolns became 46 (Lincolnshire Regiment) Anti-Aircraft Battalion, one of its officers, Lt Ernest Piggott-Smith commanding a detachment representing Grimsby at the Coronation of King George VI in London in 1937. Piggott-Smith, later Major, concluded World War Two as town major of Rome, his CO, Lt Colonel Cecil Franklin, concluding

Embussed. Lt Cecil Franklin (centre) trawler owner, later Colonel and town major of Schleswig. The picture was taken in the 1920s in Eleanor Street.

his as town major of Schleswig in North Germany. The 10th Battalion of the Lincolnshire Regiment, the Chums, was not reconstituted.

An accumulation of international events in the 1930s led Britain to be live to the possibilities of renewed war. Grimsby was again in the van of this awareness and air raid precautions, simulated air raids, the provision of air raid shelters, sirens and static water supplies had all been put in hand. The gas mask was not a mystery. As early as 1937, Home Defence companies had been formed. Grimsby had one. It was composed in the main of veterans of World War One who, on 25 August 1939 were summoned to Lincoln where they were issued with elementary items of kit, and badges, much to their disappointment, of the Leicestershire Regiment. They returned home with the brief to form a garrison company to guard the Royal Naval station's lattice masts at New Waltham. They christened themselves the Pyloneers.

Major Jack Oldroyd, Afghan War veteran and an ex-Chum.

Captain Harold Hollingsworth, ex-Lincolnshire Yeomanry, Consolidated's head salesman and director of H. Mudd Ltd.

Albert Cox in 1917, late of the Chums, ex-Archangel, mayor of Cleethorpes, a stalwart when the bugles sounded.

They included Lt John H. Hopkins, ex-5th Lincolns, solicitor, Major Charles Emerson MC ex-Chums, Captain Harold Hollingsworth ex-Lincolnshire Yeomanry, Major Jack Oldroyd ex-25th Punjabis Indian Army and an Afghan War veteran, Major Albert Cox ex-Chums who had soldiered in Archangel, the architect Fred Pye and many others, the oldest of them John Dennis who had helped to build the Louth to Mablethorpe railway line before joining the army and serving in the Zulu War of 1879! He was 84. Their service at New Waltham lasted until October 1940 when the unit was 'stood down', several of its members going on to serve in other capacities in other units, particularly the Home Guard. Within 48 hours of Chamberlain's sombre pronouncement on 3 September 1939, 900 men besieged Grimsby Borough Police Station in search of worthwhile roles. They were of all ages and experiences and within hours there were patrols in operation on Grimsby golf course and the Marsh railway yards. Captain Frank Evison, ex-4th Lincolns and the RAF, was appointed recruiting officer.

On 14 May 1940, the Local Defence Volunteers were formed, its title changed at the instigation of Winston Churchill to the Home Guard in July. Grimsby's 900, now much swelled, were formed into three battalions, the 5th Lindsey covering Grimsby, the 6th Lindsey covering Cleethorpes and the 7th Lindsey patrolling surrounding areas. Old American

May 1944 and the mayor, Councillor Max (front left) on the town hall steps. The District CO, Colonel Pugh, takes the salute with Grimsby's town major Major Peter Green behind him and Mrs Bloom. The familiar figure of Supt Birtles, with a sword, is on the right.

Ross rifles and denim uniforms with which they were first issued were replaced by better things as the months went by. The 5th Lindsey had four main companies and there were others, almost private, formed by Spiller's flour mills, the staff of Consolidated Trawlers, the gas company, electricity board and the waterworks.

Dr Barrowman became MO and the commanding officer was that ex-gunner Lt Colonel John Hinton a well known dentist. Captain Ernest Potter, ex-HAC and Legion of Frontiersmen, commanded a company. Armed with a miscellany of weapons which included the Blacker Bombard, they even formed a coastal artillery unit using the improvised Smith Gun which could be towed behind an Austin Seven – but had to be tipped on its side to fire its 10lb shell 1,000 yards, the wheel become a swivel. Grimsby's Home Guard was far from casual. Several of its members were mentioned in despatches and three of them, Lt E.J.W. Waters, Pte C.R. Roberts and Pte K.W. Stockdale were killed in one of the many air raids on the town.

Grimsby was spared the devastation meted out to Hull but was nonetheless hammered. The well documented anti-personnel butterfly bomb raid of 14 June 1943 in which 99 people were killed in

Major William Michael Lambert Smethurst (extreme right) shortly before his death in America, whence he had emigrated in the 1970s. He won his MC with the 4th Indian Division in 1945.

Grimsby and Cleethorpes did not thrust the town into the headlines as the matter was hushed up in the interests of security. Indeed Grimsby thought it was unique in being the depository for butterfly bombs for many years afterwards. It wasn't. On this occasion, the town was sealed off by Royal Engineer bomb disposal squads and semi-martial law prevailed for several days.

Invasion of the east coast was considered a likelihood but Grimsby and its environs were apparently well defended. Two 6in guns were installed on the fish docks' North Wall and manned by 318 Coast Battery Royal Artillery and, once again, an armoured train roamed the railway lines with, variously, 1914–18 six-pounder or 12ins howitzers manned by a mix of gunners and Royal Marines. In truth, Grimsby was probably undefendable.

A leaflet was distributed to local people. 'An invasion committee has been formed. Everyone must stand firm against the invader. Do nothing rash or provocative and take no foolish risks. But do not miss any chance of injuring or disposing of an enemy.' Faced with such problems the population tended to stand and stare at the sky. But Grimsby coped.

At its helm was the town major, the reassuring figure of Major Peter Green, ex-Argyll and Sutherland Highlanders, a 1914–18 veteran who conducted Grimsby's defences from a small office in Abbey Drive West and slept in his own bed in Bargate Avenue. And in his office on the docks, the fishing company chief Carl Ross composed news letters to all members of his staff serving all over the world – and banged up in German POW camps – keeping them in touch with local events, never in any doubt as to the war's outcome. Of his fellow company director Mr Ross wrote, tongue in cheek: 'Major Green is now the town major and concerned with the defences of the area. I understand in this respect the company are to have no privileges.'

And when it was all over, so they returned, this time Major Michael Smethurst with an MC and Captain Mark Wintringham with an MC (like his father before him). And once again there was that shared feeling of pride which permeated the town.

And Major John West came home after serving in 60th Field Regiment, Royal Artillery, the Grimsby gunners and heirs to that same regiment which Colonel Tonge had commanded in World War One… and whose legal practice he now resumed. And they, all of them, had their own horrors to forget. But for them the peace was to be long-lived. Little good comes of war, even for the victors.

Major John West who served in the heir to Colonel Tonge's artillery regiment and returned to Grimsby to resume Colonel Tonge's former solicitors' practice.

But the end of World War Two brought a bonus for Grimsby. When, in 1939, the Germans comprehensively overran Poland, temporarily sharing the spoils with Russia, a number of Polish soldiers escaped the armies of both their enemies, fleeing their stricken country and, via the Carpathian mountains, reached a haven of sorts in the Middle East and Palestine. Many of these men were cavalrymen – Poland had 33 regiments of horsed

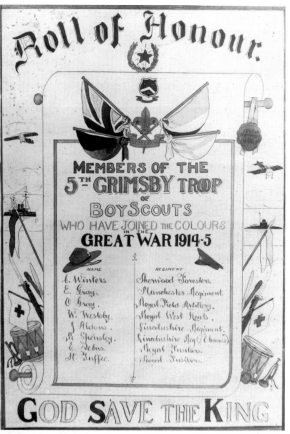

A reminder of sacrifice – the roll-call of the 5th Scartho Boy Scouts, revealing the diversity of regiments in which Grimsby boys served.

cavalry in 1939 – and, grouping together and titling themselves The Carpathian Lancers, formed part of a Polish Brigade of inestimable benefit to the Allied Command. Given the horses of the recently mechanised Royal Scots Greys, they fought, first, in North Africa before winning an imperishable reputation in the Italian campaign, their fighting at Monte Cassino assuring them of immortality.

But there were to be few rewards for these gallant men at the war's end when their homeland was annexed by the USSR and vanished behind the Iron Curtain. Fortunately for Grimsby, the Carpathian Lancers were brought to the town for demobilisation and here – often for want of anywhere else to go – about 50 or 60 of the 40 officers and 700 men stayed. Men of such calibre and grit fitted as a piece of a jigsaw into the framework of the town and, despite language difficulties, embraced the natives and were embraced in turn. Their commanding officer, Lt Colonel Stanislaw Wyskota-Zakrzewski DSO, a delightful and very handsome man, was among those who stayed, solicitous for his men, now civilians, to the end of his days. He died, aged 84, in 1986.

An immediately pre-war awareness that things could turn nasty resulted in the training of children in the use of the gas-mask... but without the benefit of actually missing school. Note, too, the poster on the wall of this Nunsthorpe school classroom advocating the benefits of emigration to America, New Zealand, Australia, China... and Japan.

The other provision against calamity at Nunsthorpe School and elsewhere was the erection of air-raid shelters, these four schoolgirls having just explored the interior. All too soon the shelters were to be in earnest use.

Heralds of the New World, a substantial squad of Germany's elite visited Grimsby on a round-Britain tour (recce?). Twenty members of the then-celebrated Hitler Youth paid a visit to the town and were captured on film by Harold Hillam as they paused for thought in Victoria Street. In the photograph above one of the Borough force keeps a proprietorial eye on proceedings as they pose in some disarray outside the Prudential Assurance Company offices.

Below, at the River Head, they posed in a more orderly shot against the backdrop of the Imperial Furnishing Company and with Duttons the outfitters at the New Street corner. Each of their belt buckles bears the swastika badge. All wear khaki shirts with black shorts, all their cycles are identical and all the riders bear a distinct resemblance to each other.

In 1937 members of the Hitler Youth, heirs to Germany's branch of the Scout movement paid a visit to the annual camp at Cherry Garth in Humberston Avenue, home of Colonel J.W. Wintringham who was the county commissioner for Boy Scouts. Their uniforms, all black, bear a sinister resemblance to other black uniforms worn by members of the German armed forces and their belt buckles reveal a single letter S as a lightning flash.

The war years proved disruptive both to Grimsby and elsewhere when fear of bombing forced the older to consider the younger... and a policy of evacuation was forced on many cities, especially ports. These two pictures reveal the departure from the scene of boys from Armstrong Street school on the West Marsh, gas masks round their necks, small suitcases in their hands, their departure supervised by seniors while little sisters look on in a mix of amusement, vexation and sadness.

It was the MS & L which initiated the ferry service whereby the three-mile journey from New Holland to Hull could be effected, and built a railway to New Holland for Grimsby people. Many shallow draught paddle steamers then plied the waters of which the last, the Castle class, are best recalled. Their immediate precursors were the *Brocklesby*, the *Cleethorpes* and this one, the *Killingholme*, seen here in 1936. She it was which had carried King George V and Queen Mary at the opening of the Immingham Dock in 1912, although she was then painted white. Withdrawn from her passenger-carrying role in 1939, PS *Killingholme* became the depot ship to the barrage balloon section of the RAF during the whole of World War Two. She was then scrapped and replaced (specifically) by PS *Tattershall Castle*, built at West Hartlepool in 1934.

Grimsby, having (secretly) been deemed undefendable, a series of so-called 'Stop Lines' were detailed to the west of the town, the first being the line of Barton Street. Beyond this declivity lurked, at Caistor and Brocklesby the 1st Derbyshire Yeomanry whose collection of odd vehicles included a Peerless armoured car, allegedly a museum exhibit recalled to use. This artists' impression is of the reception the Panzers would have met had Grimsby been over-run. The leading vehicles are Standard Beaverette Mark I light reconnaissance cars – 14hp Standards with armourplate and weighing two tons, a Bren-gun carrier on the right and an American saloon car on the left with a Bren-gunner standing in the boot. Behind, infantry is being disgorged from Granville Tours buses. Could the Panzers have possibly succeeded?

Lt Colonel Stanislaw Wyskota-Zakrzewski, the epitome of the beau sabreur, born 1902 and commissioned at the age of 18 into the crack 17th Lancers, Polish Army. He fought, with the drawn sword against Budenny's Bolshevik cavalry horde at the Battle of Warsaw in 1920 and went on to command the Carpathian Lancers and become part of the British Guards Armoured Brigade, winning the DSO and the Virtuti Militare (first class). In Grimsby he became a founder of the town's Abbey Group of artists and died in 1986, mourned by his men, remembered by his adoptive town, a gallant man.

EXODUS

ENGLISH commercial myth has it that it is the first generation which makes the money, the second which spends it and the third which is left to reap a slender harvest. Thus, here in Grimsby as elsewhere, the saying 'clogs to clogs in three generations' was to prove true or false – the footwear having peculiar relevance because of the requirements of the pontoon. Grimsby was, by the 1960s and 70s a four-generation town.

But Grimsby's demise was not of its making and it may take comfort from this. Grimsby's first generation had been extremely determined, some of its constituents not entirely penniless, some of them entirely so. Grimsby's second generation did not squander the results of this determination but built on it, consolidated in its fathers' footsteps, although the attraction of actually going to sea in search of fish did lose its allure.

Fishing, especially in sailing smacks, is not fun, not glamorous. And life on the fish docks is without charm. Although sea-going was in the blood – and some continued to do so to the end – the ability by this second generation to pay other people to do the fishing for them was surely irresistible. It availed itself. There is nothing more natural. And many of these employed people ultimately rose to a prosperity equal, if not superior, to those who employed them.

Much has been written – and continues to be written – concerning the 'fate' of lads employed as deckhands on Grimsby fishing smacks during the period 1870 to 1890. They have been portrayed as victims of cruel masters, victims, too, of a system where every hand was agin them and the law connived in unison in making their lives a misery. Few of them were native. Most were imported and often from workhouses and orphanages. Many were on the parish. With the enormous benefit of hindsight, 21st-century man regards them as put upon, mistreated and so on.

In Britain in 1870 boys were no longer up chimneys. But in the coal mines and in the sweat shops of East London, of Birmingham, Manchester and the industrial North and Scotland, poor lads got a raw deal. It was, however regrettable, a norm and it was reflected to a lesser extent in the services where drummer boys and 'powder monkeys' served, under fire, in the battles which established the British Empire. But few were the poor boys eventually to own a coal mine or a factory.

In Grimsby, skippers, often kindly, sometimes childless and frequently deeply religious, gave these poor lads a billet and a start in life which they would not have enjoyed had they remained in Stepney and Bow. And although there are some well-documented – and frequently aired – examples of cruelty and abuse, Grimsby's 'poor lads' often prospered and found in this generous town a new life and a fulfilment they would not have otherwise encountered.

Many modern Grimbarians have extremely fresh memories of wealthy Grimsby skippers in their new cars and accompanied by their equally prosperous looking wives in their fur coats. And what other

It is hard to believe that these strong, handsome and well set-up chaps are the ill-treated and disaffected. And they are not. These are Grimsby fishermen, all fired with the will to work and succeed, smart, and one or two of them proudly wearing the uniform of the part-time Militia of which they were frequently members.

English working man than the Grimsby fisherman regularly used taxis to get himself to work?

Every one of these successful men had 'come up the hard way' and none would deny their good fortune. And then there was education, education provided, education self-applied or education at a boarding establishment. The first was increasingly available, the second eagerly sought where the desire was present and the third took its recipients beyond the borough boundaries and to a world beyond the pontoon.

And it was through a combination of application and success that the gradual exodus from Grimsby began. Initially the distancing was merely physical – from New Clee and Harrington Street – to Heneage Road or to Abbey Park Road and then, ever accelerating, to Scartho and Humberston and well beyond… to the countryside proper and to matters far removed from the sea and from fishing – to farming.

Trawler owners and one-time smack owners became farmers in quantity, often merely by purchase, visiting their new holdings in their new motor cars, not putting hand to the plough. And the grand country house began to appeal. Where one was available it was bought. Where not, one was built.

All these pictures came from an exceptional presentation album given to Mr Orby Bradley, local coal merchant and worthy and chairman of the Grimsby Fisherlads' Institute, on his retirement from it in 1910.

The Marsdens, Huddersfield accountants who had consolidated Sir George Doughty's several interests, owned or lived in, at different times, three – Panton, Wykeham and Thorpe, near Louth.

Neal (Cornelius) Green, fish curer and smack owner, had two – Halstead and Holbeck, and described himself, by 1935, as a farmer. Markham Cook (trawlers) went to Sausthorpe. The Ticklers (jam) to Bradley Manor, the Bacons (trawling) to Scartho, the Doughtys to Waltham. Sir George Sleight built Weelsby as the Dixons (paper making) built the Lutyens-designed house, The Gairs, at Bradley. In modern times the Parkes (trawlers) built at Kirmond-le-Mire.

And with the purchase came the involvements and distractions of rural life ...shooting, hunting, coursing and an association with the surviving squirearchy grateful for this new involvement and infusion of finance. The Charltons (engineering) went to Elkington Hall and the Dobsons (trawling) bought the house later. None of those whose family origins were in smack fishing so embraced farming – and so excelled at it in all its complexity as did Sir Joseph Nickerson, whose reputation became international. But although the most famous he was but one of many.

The Butts and the Crampins, the Baskcombs, the Bannisters and the Lamberts (all trawling) went

Where there was no house, they built one. This is Enfield House, quite the most remarkable of all the many mansions built in Humberston Avenue by Grimsby trawler owners. Erected in three stages by George Lowe Alward, the glass-sided tower housed four large telescopes. Alward numbered astronomy among his many interests... and could use the 'scopes to see his trawlers on the not-too-distant Humber. The house was completed in 1903 and demolished between the wars.

Panton Hall near Wragby, an early 18th-century house in which Nicholas Hawksmoor had a considerable hand, was one of the Marsden's several houses. It was demolished about 1960.

Halstead Hall near Stixwould, Woodhall Spa was the first of Neal Green's purchases, a remarkable survivor which, largely thanks to him, still stands.

farming. And, as they went, so their trawling firms either merged or closed or amalgamated to form giant amorphous combines. The country life was also seen as ideal for others less fortunate and Harry Markham Cook acquired both Lynwode Manor, near Market Rasen, and North Ormsby Manor as rural homes for 24 fishermen's orphans.

The licensed trade also had a great appeal and into it, as enthusiasts, went many concerned with smacks, including the Evisons, Guzzwells, Butts, Forges, Brownes and Hill (the trawler owner rather than the mineral water maker of the same name).

Newspaper ownership also had an attraction and the Doughtys, Baskcombs, Easons, Barkers and, most successfully, the Wintringhams all at one time or another became editor-proprietors.

In addition to education – and with it the urge to consider 'higher things' – came three more invitations to sever connection with Grimsby.

Although World War One had offered Grimsby men little more than a glimpse of a filthy trench in Flanders, World War Two widened many a young man's horizons. The Pacific, Canada, South Africa, India, continental Europe and beyond revealed other people's lives, ambitions, landscapes... and all far removed from Fish Dock Road.

Secondly there was marriage. Until the 1930s Grimsby people had married Grimsby people – perforce. Families became closely inter-related and intertwined. A foolish stranger to the town speaking disparagingly of a person might discover to his embarrassment and cost that he was addressing that person's cousin or his brother-in-law. It often happened. Families became great extensions of chapel and commercial life. Cleethorpes was even more clannish in this respect. But post-war mores were to decree that such complex dynasties would be stretched – often to breaking point – when other allegiances in the south of England or abroad came into the picture.

Thirdly the post-war years brought to Grimsby, as elsewhere, a revolution in business and commerce. And it was this revolution that was to put an end to Grimsby's self-made independence and structure. The collapse of the fishing industry is a subject so well-documented as to need little elaboration in these pages. A combination of circumstances far beyond the control of any Grimsby man, or any Grimsby commercial concern, resulted in trawling being abandoned. Despite the resting of the North Sea between 1939 and 1945 and maybe because of the post-war boom in fishing, North Sea stocks dwindled due to over-fishing and insufficient care was taken to preserve stocks. The cost of oil – Grimsby's trawlers had eventually converted to oil from coal – rose to prohibitive levels and was determined on an international market.

Finally, the imposition of fishing limits by both European mainland countries and, particularly, Iceland, denied waters once haunted by Grimsby ships and even promoted a 'cod war' with Iceland. Fishing the oceans as we had known it for a century was over.

The post-war years were, too, the years of the takeover bid, of asset-stripping, of international combines. Those of Grimsby's businesses not concerned with fishing did not escape this whirl-wind. Chain stores took over local stores, sometimes closing them down sometimes substituting their names.

There were many such casualties. Ticklers' jam factory relocated and then was bought out. Hewitt's brewery was taken over and closed down. Dixons the paper millers, following a major fire, closed. Grimsby's solitary attempt to produce its own motor car, the Lloyd, foundered. And what few

Holbeck Manor, considerably larger and equally exceptional, became the depository for Mr Green's assiduous gleanings of architectural fragments, relics built into the fabric or re-erected in the romantic grounds and gardens.

The interior of Kirmond Hall built for the Parkes family in 1975 and designed by George Palejowski, one of the Carpathian Lancers to settle in Grimsby and prosper.

remaining manufacturing chemists there were closed or sold up.

In the large number of deep-freezing plants, all established to assist the fishing industry, was some local salvation found, and these were adapted to suit a changing world and embraced the on-the-doorstep farm produce from the county, thus re-establishing a link with Lincolnshire which the town had not needed for 100 years.

The importance of freezing to the history of Grimsby cannot be overstated. Initially, that is to say in the 1860s, ice was imported from Norway and brought here in ice-barques. The business was managed by the Great Grimsby Ice Company which supervised its discharge at a berth alongside the slipway at the north end of the Royal Dock. About 1870 the Grimsby Co-operative Ice Company was formed and, from the same Norwegian source, ice came ashore near the graving dock entrance. But Grimsby determined to make its own ice and, by 1890, at the corner of Victoria Street and Corporation Road and opposite the Palace Theatre, an ice factory, initially run by a Mr Molyneux and then a Mr Naylor opened for business producing 25 tons of it in 24 hours. The days of the barques was almost over. The factory was taken over by the Great Grimsby Ice Company and the Co-operative which then combined.

Hagerup and Doughty then opened their own plant and finally the Standard Ice Factory, was opened by the Butts in Victor Street after the 1914–18 war and cost more than £1million. Many trawler owners were deeply involved in ice production, particularly Sir Alec Black who, in 1939, bought the Standard Ice firm from the Butts. Today it is no exaggeration to say that freezing is a *sine qua non* of Grimsby's enormous food producing capacity.

The development of the Humber Bank heralded the arrival of a swathe of new Grimbarians, filling a void by apparent natural succession. But old Grimsby seemed like a husk. The subsequent closure of the Grimsby to Peterborough railway line in the 1970s had a deep significance, for it had been the vein through which Grimsby's lifeblood had flowed to London and the South East. It was the throughfare upon which Grimsby's claim to be the greatest fishing port in the world had matured.

Then Grimsby lost its County Borough status and

Elkington Hall, the Smyth family seat, an Italianate confection built in 1842 was acquired first by the Charltons and then the trawler-owning Dobsons and demolished in the 1970s.

with it its independence, which included its police force and general control over all its affairs. Then it was further deemed not to be part of Lincolnshire, but of a new and generally unwelcome mass to be called Humberside. The great days were gone. There were no trawlers and the once well-known names of the town's principals faded in importance and disappeared.

Charles Dobson (1888–1969), proprietor of the Dobson Steam Fishing Company and the Albion Steam Fishing Company. He was the son of Charles Henry Dobson (1858–1932) who went to the country in 1938 founding the 5,000-acre Elkington Estates near Louth. At the time he lived at The Cedars, Louth. The Dobsons were prominent in Grimsby affairs, Alderman George Shelton Dobson was mayor in 1891, the year of the founding of the Albion S.F. Co of which he was a director.

Both the village of Scartho – finally incorporated into the Borough of Grimsby in 1927 – and the developed farmland at what became known as Nunsthorpe, allowed Grimsby room to spread, and its citizens to move out of the old town. Scartho epitomised 'the country' and the road to it began to be built upon in 1904. Two trawler owners immediately built substantial houses on it. The road left town, passing Scartho's Victorian tower windmill and E. W. Farebrother's workhouse-infirmary, and emerged into a place of thatched cottages and quaint streets, with an ancient church and a wholly rural economy.

This was swiftly transformed by Grimsby people into a Home Counties annexe with a mock-Tudor garage and

The road to Scartho was the principal escape route from Grimsby, the first houses to be built on it seen on the left in 1907.

shops to match, ribbon development linking it to Nuns' Corner and continuing on to the borough boundary where the green fields resumed. Much of the developed land at Scartho belonged to the Earl of Yarborough – whose family crest still embellishes one or two surviving estate cottage gables – and development was seemly and agreeable and, as perceived then, rural in character. Today it is merely suburban.

An attempt in 1904 to build a substantial public house in the village – to be called Ingle Nook – which would cater for 'a better class of person' failed. The previous village pub, The Gate, had closed in the 1860s for want of custom. Those in charge of the new Scartho denied there was any new need of a pub however smart. It was to be many years before one did open its doors and Scartho, to this day, retains the atmosphere of a village.

Nunsthorpe was an entirely different expansion. Following World War One it was determined – in line with a well known exhortation from Lloyd George –

to provide new and very good accommodation for those returning to civilian life from the army and, in Grimsby, from service at sea. A group of Grimsby architects, led by John Cresswell and Herbert Scaping, banded together, sinking all rivalry, to create a small Garden City on 128 acres of farmland also owned by the Earl of Yarborough.

The need for the houses was greater because of the poor – even squalid – condition of some houses in old Grimsby. There would be 993 houses, 12 shops, allotments, a new school... and a church. By 1923 138 houses had been erected. But by 1928 work petered out. By then known as the Laceby Road Housing Scheme it quickly revived and Nunsthorpe, as it had been named, received a fillip with the building of the new and very large school – designed by Herbert Scaping and opened in September 1931.

It was, they said, 'a school in a garden' and cost £30,000. There were 900 pupils and room for a further 400.

The place was light and airy and partly single-

Scartho Road's first marker – one passed as hastily as possible – was the workhouse infirmary, one of Ernest Farebrother's commissions and built in 1892. Facing it, ominously, the 'new' cemetery was opened in 1889, also a Farebrother work.

storeyed, with acres of windows and a substantial playground. Compared with most inner-Grimsby schools it was revolutionary.

Nunsthorpe's church, St Martin's – named after the patron saint of soldiers – was built and opened in 1937 and was said by a contemporary critic to resemble a razor blade factory. Before its consecration services had been held, since 1922, in a purpose-built wooden mission church built by Mr Markwell Holmes, who did much building for Lord Yarborough. It is still there, and it gave birth to St Martin's School, now on Bargate, which held its first classes in it.

After the intervention of World War Two, building resumed at Nunsthorpe and it was to be the only recipient in the town of pre-fabricated houses – soon abbreviated – and very popular they were. Several survive. For many thousands of people, the expansion afforded by Scartho and Nunsthorpe –

and the Gilbey-owned Little Coates estate – was a springboard for further distancing and soon neighbouring villages, especially Waltham and Humberston became Grimsby's dormer suburbs.

It is true that some did move back, for the terraced housing they had left became cheaper than the 'country' homes they sought. But, generally speaking, the move out of town was unstoppable. Grimsby had ceased to be a close community. The old birds had flown and left behind them derelict nests which were adapted for use by the lame and the aged.

Today the old establishment lives in America, Geneva, the Home Counties, Scotland, the West Country, South Africa. Some have turned their backs on the past. Some relish contact and speak wistfully of decades past. Some revisit and are saddened by what has transpired in their absence. But all recognise progress when they see it, whatever they may think of it.

The road's next milestone was cheerily rural, the tower mill of 1869, with five sweeps and in good order. It was to survive until the 1950s.

And then it was all ribbon development to Scartho, an inter-war highway to heaven. Although the village was incorporated into the Borough in 1927, Scartho still offered village life and big trees.

And a small ancient church, St Giles's eventually proved too small and was enlarged.

An early development was Pelham Avenue, as delightful a slice of *rus in urbe* as could be conceived.

The village soon had a mock-Tudor garage and mock-Tudor shops and the Home Counties atmosphere was in the making.

By 1910 there were so many children in Scartho that a new council school was built and opened by Mrs William Hitzen, wife of the German Consul in Grimsby. The village had never had a school before. Until 1910, 100 children made a daily trek into Grimsby for lessons.

On the Waltham Road, however, little had changed by 1938. Dixon's Farm, the roof glimpsed over the pavement-side barns and its attendant outbuildings and cottages, still stood where they had for a century. The farmhouse is now a hotel and the barns and cottages have been cleared for a car park and a doctor's surgery.

The other side of the road, despite a row of Edwardian villas, still sported end-on cottages with roses round the door. Today a supermarket and attendant shops – and another car park – take their place.

While Holmes the bakers made their doorstep deliveries by van, greengroceries came on the hoof, Benny Atkin, who lived in an eight-foot off the Waltham Road – where he kept his horse – made his rounds the old fashioned way. And you could stop him and buy one.

Scartho continued until it could do so no more, the bungalows and semis petering out at the Borough boundary.

John Cresswell (1857–1944) architect.

Nunsthorpe was the Brave New World, not of cosy cottages and country lanes and Saxon towers, but of modernity and escape from the close-packed and grimy terraces of both the East and the West Marshes. This was the Garden City – and was known as such for years – with generous roads (in the absence of motor cars) broad grass verges, serried trees, well lit at night. In this study, with young Grimsby looking on, the tower of the infirmary can be seen in the right distance.

The pre-fab was a hallmark of Nunsthorpe, popular, easy to erect, cheap, enduring... and still there.

St Martin's Church, apogee of modern architecture, was named after the patron saint of soldiers for Nunsthorpe, which it served, was originally meant for returned soldiers from World War One. Designed by Lawrence Bond and consecrated in 1937 it is, suitably, concrete and brick, light and airy, bright and breezy, an echo of its time.

Nunsthorpe had a school, not for 100 children as in Scartho, but for hundreds and hundreds, a school, like its houses and church, light and airy with lots and lots of glass and windows wide open, a healthy school, even better than Armstrong Street on the West Marsh which, itself, was splendid enough.

It was a vigorous school...

...a school where small children sat in fresh air and in small groups...

...and where free school meals were provided, here, for the first time, in 1937.

And supervising and teaching Young Grimsby were, back row left to right: Messrs Allan, Williams, Bell, Farrow, Callaghan, Davies, Wilkinson; centre row: Messrs Galloway, Robins, Wainman, Pendegrass, Manders; front row: Mr Webb, Mrs Pendegrass, Messrs Hodgson, Kingsland, Mrs Broth (school secretary), Messrs Hillam and Gambrell.

LAMENTATIONS

ALTHOUGH the English don't mind living in houses which are centuries old, they demur at working in archaic premises. So that while private houses remain, public ones become obsolete and disused. Grimsby, which was quickly built in the space of 80 years, became a classic, if modest, late Victorian town with all the charm and all the vulgarity which 'late-Victorian' architecture implies.

In the 1930s one or two architectural interlopers appeared, notably the Central Hall, built in the tradition established at Wembley Stadium – the Imperial Furnishing Company's River Head premises (all Crittall windows and whitewash) and the two monster cinemas, the Regal in Freeman Street and the Ritz at Cleethorpes and both opened in 1937. Forfeited to make way for them were the Italianate Duncombe Street Wesleyan chapel (1873) and the Prince of Wales' Theatre.

In 1925, Woolworth's moved from their first Cleethorpe Road shop to open a modern store in Freeman Street, and bought and demolished Zion

Queen Street, Grimsby in 1942 revealing the one-storey character of the town's terraced housing. This is the corner with Holme Street.

Peppercorn Walk, by the side of the Doughty Road subway declivity in 1938. Most was forfeit to bombing.

Baptist Chapel, built in 1868 and spiritual home to many early settlers here. Thus it was, even before the war, that Grimsby's robust Victorian entity began to disappear. As Victorian buildings were not regarded as important, and were, indeed, decried, this was all seen as progress.

The war years, and the bombing, cleared more of this character and, when the war was over and when Victorian had become a word of pure vilification, there were no voices raised in protest. Public buildings, when they have outlived their original purpose, seldom lend themselves to other use. And when other, major pressures are applied, their removal from the scene become easier.

The five major pressures, which were to deprive the barely-mature town of what identity it had, were increased motor traffic, a falling-off in church and chapel attendance, the effects of television, the closure of businesses and a borough planning committee strapped for space, hemmed in and confined in its borough boundary.

Of course such pressures exerted themselves across England. Grimsby was not alone in feeling their pinch. But Grimsby was unique in that most towns owed their appearance to other centuries than merely the 19th. Quick to go – and for several reasons – were the Church Extension Society Anglican churches. St Stephen's (1914) in Grant Thorold Park was built on faulty foundations and had posed a structural problem for a long time. St Andrew's Freeman Street (1870) also had flawed foundations, having been built in an area once riven by ditches and drains. In any event Grimsby is notorious in parts for its geological faults. Both churches, closed to their congregations for some time, were pulled down.

All Saint's Heneage Road (1905) survived damage by the Luftwaffe but was finally cleared, having become derelict, in recent times. St Paul's West Marsh (1888) went with its entire surroundings in the 1970s. St John's Cleethorpe Road, a very large church built in 1877 to serve the burgeoning New Clee, and James Fowler's only Grimsby church, was demolished in 1982 in the interests of road

The demolition of Grimsby in the wake of its commercial decline was, in part, verging on the wilful. This is the Manse for the Hainton Square chapel minister, allowed to fall into dereliction and then, having become an eyesore, demolished.

widening. St Luke's, Heneage Road (1912), was cleared in 1969. The sole survivor of Grimsby's Anglican revival is St Barnabas, King Edward Street (1900). This is now a warehouse. Thus perished the inheritance of Canon Robert Ainslie and his successor Canon Young.

The same desperate fate awaited Grimsby's many Nonconformist chapels, some of which – in a strongly Nonconformist town – were splendid. Among the first to go was the spectacular Hainton Square Primitive Chapel, built in 1875, and which could have graced a Roman Forum. Hainton Square was, at one time, the third most important meeting of roads, yielding only to the Old Market Place and Riby Square. Here were villas and doctor's surgeries, the old established (1877) Cyclists' Club (you see

from this date alone that 'old' in Grimsby is not 'old' as York or Hull or Lincoln understand 'old'), the splendid Municipal College in Eleanor Street, and the mansions of trawler owners and mayors and councillors. A commonplace concrete block of offices and shops replaced the chapel.

Although the man in the street does not go about articulating his feelings, the removal of Hainton Square Chapel affected this mythical chap, whether he was a member of its congregation or not. The Victoria Wesleyan Chapel on Cleethorpe Road sported one of Grimsby's spires – a feature with which the town was never over-endowed. It was built in 1860 and had become familiar. After a sad spell as an employment exchange and stripped of its embellishment, it was pulled down.

Freeman Street, despite attempts to give Victor Street added importance, remained to the end the highway to the docks. In the main it was single storey, but the Regal Cinema on the right became, and remains, a dominant feature. The removal of St Andrew's Church spire was a blow.

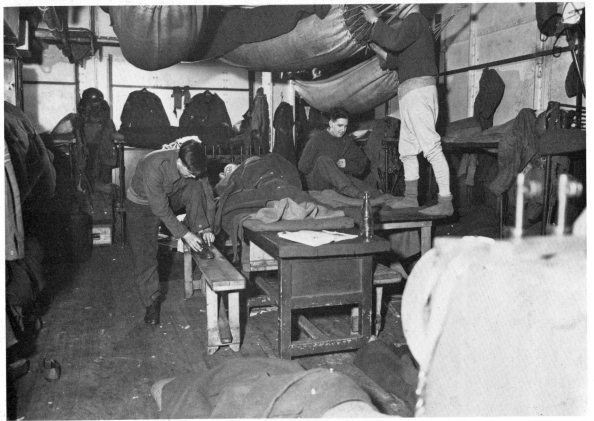

116. Soldiers in hammocks. As can be seen the accommodation on the forts had a Spartan flavour about it, and life could be monotonous especially when heavy weather cut links with the mainland.

117. Conways of Cleethorpes to the rescue!

114. Haile and Bull Sands forts, off Grimsby, were under the control of Northern Command and manned by 274 and 275 Batteries of the 513th Coast Regiment, Royal Artillery. The photograph was taken on 11 February 1942 by Lieutenant O'Brien.

115. A gun crew at action stations, 11 February 1942.

112. The destroyer HMS *Scorpion* leads a sub-division of the 23rd Flotilla round the Humber Lightship.

113. Saturday night at New Waltham Royal Naval Wireless Station. This photograph was taken in February 1943 and shows staff at the station together with wives and friends at one of the regular social nights held in the canteen.

HMS Grimsby

During the grim week following the retreat in Greece, the loss of Crete and the German advance across North Africa towards Egypt and the Suez Canal, the isolated fortress of Tobruk held out and came under a siege that was to last for 242 days. That Tobruk held out for so long was due both the determination of the defending garrison and the Royal Navy whose main task was to bring in supplies of sto. es, food, petrol and ammunition.

On 25 May 1941, HMS *Grimsby* and the South African armed whaler *Southern Maid*, were en route to Tobruk escorting the SS *Helka* which was carrying a cargo of petrol and water, when they were attacked by Stuka dive-bombers. Bombs were dropped near the *Helka* and *Grimsby* and the *Southern Maid* was machine-gunned though she in turn hit two of her attackers.

Two hours later, the *Luftwaffe* returned. The *Helka* was hit by two bombs and broke in half. The aft section of the ship (where the engines were) continued to sail on. The forepart remained afloat with most of the crew clinging to it. Having stopped the engines, boats were lowered and the crew rescued.

The *Grimsby* shot down two aircraft before she too was bombed and sunk. All this time the *Southern Maid* put up an intense anti-aircraft barrage and succeeded in bringing down one aircraft and damaging several others. When the *Luftwaffe* withdrew she picked up the survivors and made for Mersa Matruh. *Right: Grimsby,* having been hit, begins to settle in the water. *Below: Grimsby* is down by the stern. On the right in the background is the bow section of the *Helka*.

Flottergate Primitive was, perhaps, the best built of all, a tour-de-force, erected by George Doughty's building company and spiritual focus for many prominent in the town. Its interior, of the best pitch pine the Baltic countries could (ill) afford, it lasted longest and was a victim of Top Town redevelopment to make way for Mammon in the shape of shopping precincts and car parks.

In the body of Ebenezer Primitive Chapel on Cleethorpe Road lay the very soul of New Clee Methodism, the essence of happiness for the many smack owners and skippers who had found landfall in Grimsby. For years, those who had originally been members of its congregation, despite having moved away from New Clee, continued to travel in to town to attend its services. It was pulled down in 1968 to make way for Asda's first provision store, a proviso being that the store could not sell alcohol. It was a proviso accepted. But in future, supermarkets found sites where such strictures were not imposed.

Arlington Street and Garibaldi Street chapels had already succumbed and the loss of the Baptist Tabernacle in Victoria Street, built in 1877 and a masterpiece for John Brown the eminent (Baptist)

And this, once a simple farmhouse became, following embellishment by the Wintringham family, The Abbey, in capacious grounds and with a primitive swimming pool. It was demolished for new estates of houses.

Frederick Fields Lord owned The Bon Marche, a large haberdashery on Cleethorpe Road and is yet another of those Grimsby benefactors cheerfully forgotten by those who propound the view that Grimsby business people merely took and never gave. In his 1923 will of £40,000 he left money for the blind, the orphaned, the Wesleyans, the hospital, for children, for animals, for the Salvation Army and so on.

St Stephen's, Grant Thorold Park was begun in 1914 and built to the design of Sir W.J. Tapper and, later transformed (1934) by John Cresswell. It was a fine church, tall, bright and well supported – by its congregation but not by its foundations which were unsound. Because of this it was declared unsafe, closed and demolished.

builder, was a sad loss – especially as nothing was to occupy the site but an open space resembling a bombed site.

George Street Wesleyan, oldest established of all, built in 1847 on a timber yard, was a place of worship for many of the town's leading lights. It was replaced by a sweeping concrete block of shops and offices.

The churches and chapels were, of course, not merely buildings. They were the result of enormous fund-raising efforts, innumerable bazaars, sales-of-work, collections, of individual charity by both those who could ill afford anything and those who could donate generously. People had married in them and had their children christened in them. Funerals had been held in them and many had attended attached schools, or at least Sunday schools where Gamaliel, in many forms, had sat. Grimbarians 'belonged' to them. Speaking of individual families one would say they are 'George Street people' or 'they belong to Ebenezer'. The association was deeply felt. For Grimsby's thousands of newcomers they were the first cohesive bond, religious and social centres. And in them, friendships were formed, business partnerships were welded and love blossomed. As a generality they lasted 100 years, a short enough period for everyone to recall their origins. And when they were pulled down it was not merely the streetscape which had lost a focus of attention.

There followed the razing of the Bull Ring, most of the Old Market Place, the Grimsby General Hospital (1874), The Palace Theatre of 1904, banks, drill halls, the Gaiety Ballroom. At the same time, it was the turn of other buildings where people had gathered, the cinemas, to go. One or two survive in outline although no longer cinemas.

Then the hotels disappeared, the Ship, Flottergate, the Clee Park at New Clee among them. The stranded Corn Exchange (1854) went next having been reduced to the role of public lavatory, the Fisherlads'

The Corn Exchange, built in 1854 was one of the two buildings erected in the hope or expectation that the focus of attention for the railway company would remain in Top Town (the other was the Yarborough Hotel). But events were to prove the exchange an anachronism even in its own time. Corn exchanging soon petered out. It became an auction room.

Institute Orwell Street (1880), Hewitt's Brewery, the Masonic Hall Bethlehem Street (1877) and numerous public houses followed.

The removal of Riby Square and the subsequent clearance of Cleethorpe Road's initial north side owed everything to the installation of a belated railway line flyover. At a stroke the Royal Hotel, one of John Brown's triumphs for the MS & L went, as did all its neighbours, not least the Barrel public house. Riby Square, never a square in any event, was reduced to an inconsequence.

These public buildings were landmarks in the otherwise single-storey streets they occupied, and gave the streets the character that was, peculiarly, Grimsby's. Their replacements if any, were unbelievably banal, but were dictated by expediency and a lack of capital in the post-war town. Their disappearance was felt deeply by Grimsby people who were powerless in the face of such forces as Godlessness, to do anything about it other than write plaintive letters in the sole remaining local newspaper.

There is little doubt that one is not quite as proud of one's home town when it is so cruelly diminished.

The Corn Exchange lingered on, its Dutch Jacobethan gables a curious centrepiece. In this post-war picture the skies around it are wreathed in trolley-bus wires. It had become a public lavatory.

True this has happened elsewhere. It is a pity, nonetheless, that it had to happen so catastrophically in Grimsby. There were voices of protest. The urbane MP Anthony Crosland deplored the tally of demolition and pointed out the effect on the streetscape of the removal of its principal landmarks. But his observations won the vociferous scorn of the town council.

A Civic Society was set up in the 1960s when the scale of change became apparent and when plans for more of it were revealed. It was headed by the same Peter Green who had been a Ross Group director and who had been town major during the war. But for all its earnestness and promise, all its cajolery and warnings, it was powerless in the face of the causes set against it. In a few years the Society became moribund.

Hainton Street (it became an avenue in 1889) Methodist chapel, built in 1874, was a giant in a prosperous and highly respectable area of town. The trees outside had been planted in 1885.

Grimsby has now been demolished. It is only appreciated post-mortem. And 'post-mortem' is a suitable phrase with which to conclude this sad chapter. For the final example – and the worst – of the erasure of Grimsby's Victorian past was the needless clearance of the nine-acre Doughty Road cemetery. This 1855 necropolis, established early in Grimsby's growth, was much more than a cemetery, more than an 'estate'. It was a document. It was also a very fine, very sombre and very typical record of the comings and the goings of all those who had made the town what it was. Like St James' churchyard (which it superseded) it too was declared 'full' and was in turn followed by the Scartho Road cemetery.

Interments then petered out at Doughty Road. But following World War Two, when it was said to have become the depository for unexploded anti-personnel bombs, it was first sealed off and then cleared to become an empty space of little benefit at all to its immediate neighbourhood in particular, or to the town in general. Its demise characterises the cavalier, the mean and the casual attitude of those in authority to the urban scene. And Doughty Road cemetery was a matter over which they had full control.

George Street Wesleyan was to Grimsby's Top Town Wesleyans what St James' was to its Anglicans. It is seen here in 1850. Once again a selection of shops and offices now occupy the prominent site.

This delightful 1942 view of Victoria Street reveals the importance of spires and landmarks. The spire on the left is that of Spring Congregational chapel (1864), spiritual home of the Wintringhams. Its truncated, spireless hulk survives. The next two spires are those of the Baptist Tabernacle, opened in 1877, built by the Baptist John Brown. The chief engineer of the GNR, Richard Johnson, laid the foundation stone! It was demolished for no transparently good reason, and its vacancy remains a shattered space. Nearest to the camera is Maddison's Corner. Maddison, a Boston man, was a baker.

In fairness, some buildings do outlive their usefulness hopelessly. Such was the natural fate of the enormous Grimsby General Hospital on the West Marsh, a conglomeration, constantly added-to, which outlived its time and was pulled down with its entire surrounding district. It had once been the object of great endeavour and fund raising.

The Grosvenor Building Company, with a capital of £10,000, was registered in 1876 to buy and develop land between Dr Moody's house at the Grosvenor Street corner and the railway line. On it was built Grosvenor Terrace, the architect was Charles Bell of London, who designed Holme Hill School, seen on the back cover of this book. Among the shareholders and first residents were the mayor Thomas Charlton and Martin Maslin. Later occupants included the council's stormy petrel Isaac Watts, whose son Sidney was killed on the Somme with the Chums, and the pugilist Alderman Thomas Keetley.

The passing of the Bull Ring, at best a modest lopsided square of small shops, was much mourned. It is seen here in the late 1940s.

Victoria Wesleyan chapel was built by Grimsby's John Brown for £3,000 in 1860 on Cleethorpe Road.

The austere and Italianate Ebenezer Primitive chapel, seen here inside and out, in New Clee, served many of the early pioneers whose business was fish and whose faith was deeply Methodist. Hewins and Goodhand built it it 1870.

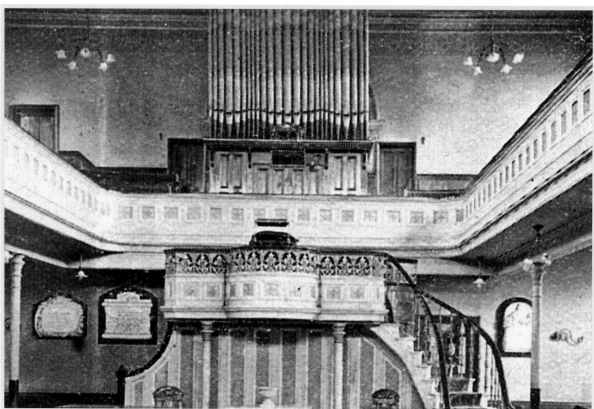

Flottergate was the biggest of the Primitive Methodist chapels, was said to have been most expensive and best built. The pitch pine interior was vast and was enhanced with painted wrought-iron fret panels round the gallery. It was demolished about 1970 to make way for the Top Town precinct of shops.

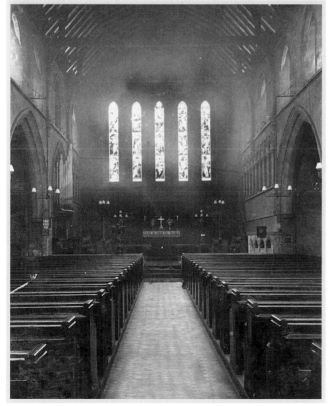

St John's New Clee, the only Grimsby church designed by James Fowler (1828–1892) was built in 1877.

Cruel blows were struck in the 1960s when, with the building of the Cleethorpe Road fly-over, the north side of Cleethorpe Road from Lock Hill to Riby Square was demolished. Forfeit were, above, the Royal Hotel, centre of attention for generations, the Royal Dock Chambers (centre) home of many commercial firms including Haddelseys the solicitors, Bannister the coal merchants, Carlboms, Hitzens, Hagerups, Bradley and so on. Demolition continued and included more modest premises including (below) the Exchange Hotel, better known as the Barrel public house, a free house and run from 1889 until 1921 by Charles Killan, grandfather of Charles Ekberg. It was a haunt of fishermen, skippers in the snug, deckhands in the public bar.

Doughty Road cemetery had no greater protagonist than Dr Walter Elwood, one of the two doctor sons of William Elwood (1852–1926) a prominent George Street Wesleyan and Victoria Street chemist for 50 years. Dr Elwood campaigned vigorously for its retention entirely on behalf of his patients many of whose relatives were buried there. His battle was long and culminated in his 'taking the council to court' in Nottingham. Regrettably he lost his action.

ACTS

At the end of the road to nowhere else and 45 miles from anywhere else of any consequence, Grimsby developed independently and almost privately. It soon had its own accent as the Devon burrs and the Essex and Kentish twangs disappeared into a uniform throaty note owing nothing to its surrounding county. Ties with places of birth were either severed, or simply withered and it was not, therefore, odd that Grimsby should develop its own interests and pursuits and fads and fancies.

Because of this remoteness, Grimsby, being small, was not on a major theatrical circuit and although some entertainers did include it on their itineraries – notably circuses and prize-fighting boxers 'fortified by drink' and billiards aces – Grimsby looked to itself to provide off-duty levity. The first amateur dramatic society was formed in the 1870s and its

Lord George Sanger's circus was well known and also visited. Here is the orchestra in an opulent coach drawn by eight skewbalds. Sanger's title was entirely self-awarded but he defied all comers to take it from him. None did. In later years Bertram Mills and Fossett's provided continuing circus thrills.

heirs, the Caxton Players continue the tradition. Grimsby has always been kind to its amateur thespians and when J. H. Curry owned and ran the Prince of Wales Theatre in Freeman Street, the only 'houses' which were guaranteed sell-outs were those when the amateurs took the stage.

The Currys, Hull people, provided through theatre and cinema, much of Grimsby's entertainment. J. H. Curry was keen to raise Grimsby's sights and put on Shakespearian productions. He even called his house in Hainton Avenue, Shakespeare House. But the plays were not a success although he persisted in the pointless struggle. But if the town was enthusiastic about the stage it was ecstatic about music and

In October 1904 Bostock and Wombwell's circus and menagerie visited Grimsby. It was not their first visit or their last. Circuses were popular attractions and B & W travelled Britain for 126 years. They set up in Freeman Street market, then an open space, with a fabulous collection of animals, the tour de force of the 1904 visit a blue-and-red-faced mandrill.

Legion are the treasured photographs of charabanc trips, coach tours and mystery outings to picturesque parts of the county and, occasionally, beyond. Grimsby's best known coach firm was Granville Tours, the older picture revealing their Pullman lounge coach with, picnic hampers on the roof grid, the lower one a Pullman-de-Luxe about to leave the Old Market Place. The lettering on their coaches was the work of a member of the Bauckham family.

innumerable ensembles, bands, orchestras and choirs – many of very long establishment – have played and sung to packed audiences for more than a century.

Their inspiration was, of course, church and chapel, particularly the latter. One celebrated journalist, Russell Spurr, briefly in Grimsby at the beginning of World War Two wrote that the town's relief came 'in singing oratorios. A couple of hours belting out the Messiah left everyone aesthetically and spiritually fulfilled.'

As a consequence of this, the town has produced some excellent choirmasters and conductors and, indeed, musicians of all sorts, particularly pianists, many of whom have played on concert platforms on the wireless and in dance bands far beyond the confines of their home town and embracing all forms of music, serious and popular.

Not that Grimsby was ever high-brow. Never... despite attempts. A classic example of attempting to 'raise the tone' is afforded by the Hall of Science, opened in Freeman Street in the early 1870s, lectures in it designed to 'elevate and develop the moral and intellectual character of the people.' Within three years it was a roller skating rink. There was, of course, a minority of interest in more academic pursuits, hence the Chess Club (1875) and, 10 years later the Grimsby Naturalists' Society. And so on.

And a vigorous town worked off its excess energy in sport – football and cricket and cycling (a club was established in 1877). Indeed so enthusiastic was the town for ball games that the prodigious Bob Lincoln wrote an entire book (*Reminiscences of Sport in Grimsby*) on the subject in 1912, pages and pages of old match reports, which found a rapt audience.

Grimsby Town Football Club (1879), originally

Although some dock-side Grimsby public houses rejoiced in the name 'hotel', many did not and were simply beer houses, four-ale bars of working town legend. Such was the Honest Lawyer in Kent Street where, about 1905 when this photograph was taken, Betsy Bentinck (left) was the licensee and her clients were fishermen old and young. Kent Street, named after Queen Victoria's father, was initial home to many who created Grimsby's prosperity, the Gidley, Jeffs, Nickerson, Greer, and Abrahams families among them.

The People's Park, a gift to the town from the Heneages, probably never had so many visitors at one time as on 6 May 1935 when the town celebrated the Silver Jubilee of the reign of George V. All the schoolchildren were marshalled. This picture was taken by Sid Burton of Wellowgate.

In parades and carnivals and school plays did Grimsby, young and old, escape from the humdrum... or float away as on this garlanded New Clee Baptists' float at the George V's Coronation festivities in 1911, pausing for the photographer in People's Park. The float won first prize.

Grimsby Pelham FC (Pelham is the surname of the Yarborough family), were admitted to the Football Alliance in 1889. Geoff Ford points out in his admirable *Grimsby Town Football Club* (Grimsby Evening Telegraph Publications 1989) that the town's geographical isolation did not make its inclusion in a national league attractive because of the travelling involved. 'Indeed to gain admission to the Alliance the club had to agree to pay half the rail fares of the visiting clubs!'

However 'Town', who were original members of the Football League's Second Division (today restyled the First with the advent of the 'Premiership') won, from the start, a loyal following and through thick and thin – the glory days of First Division fixtures (then the true top flight of the English game) in the 1930s and 1940s and the wilderness days of the 1960s – they have stayed true.

A successful football team was, and remains, an asset to a town, good for pride and morale. It is a mercy that Grimsby Town never dropped out of the Football League years ago when re-election was still possible.

Grimsby was also easily pleased, and dead whales and sheep shearing contests and rowing races (they called them regattas) and the annual Statute Fair were all events guaranteed an audience.

Like many working towns Grimsby grew up without sophistication and was to remain so... a beer and skittles town, a rough and ready mix of music hall and billiards hall and public house, a cod and chips, dig-in-the-ribs sort of a town... and none the worse for its honesty. It did not embrace the opera or ballet, or yearn for an art gallery or take any considerable interest in what are termed 'the fine arts'. It had the countryside on its doorstep and the gaudy delights of a thriving seaside resort as a neighbour and, in pigeon racing and angling and

...or in this Temperance Society's children's demonstration marching through Hainton Square in June 1914. The manse is on the right in the background.

...or in academic drama as here is 1922 where members of the cast of some long-forgotten play pose outside the Municipal College, later the Wintringham Grammar School, in Eleanor Street.

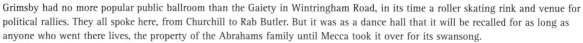

Grimsby had no more popular public ballroom than the Gaiety in Wintringham Road, in its time a roller skating rink and venue for political rallies. They all spoke here, from Churchill to Rab Butler. But it was as a dance hall that it will be recalled for as long as anyone who went there lives, the property of the Abrahams family until Mecca took it over for its swansong.

For many years the Kendal Players, named after that star of the Edwardian stage Dame Madge Kendal (1849–1935), played to packed audiences both before and after World War Two and generally in All Saints' Church Hall in Heneage Road. This scene from a production of the play *Distinguished Gathering* reveals one of the troupe's stalwarts, Myra Houldsworth. She ran the Grimsby General Hospital's registration department. She was also married to Bill, the only son of Grimsby's most interesting artist, Herbert Rollett. But she retained her maiden name. The picture over the fireplace in this set is by her father-in-law, a view of Grimsby from Cleethorpes beach. Grimsby's amateur theatricals were, in every way, home spun.

char-a-banc trips to Croxby Pond and Pelham's Pillar, it found happy relief from the hard grind of earning a Victorian living.

Grimsby was the grateful recipient of largesse from several ground landlords in the wholesome shape of parks and bowling greens and tennis courts and football pitches, of woods and walks and ponds... with all of which it was at ease.

But other gifts were received with perplexed bewilderment. The provision of a museum or art gallery in Grimsby has always been perceived by the governing council as a problem rather than an opportunity. It has not been so perceived by some outsiders or, indeed, by many ratepayers. But they have fallen into two categories – the first rural sophisticates who 'know what's good for you', with whom Grimsby has never been happy and the second a small local minority dismissed as being 'arty-crafty'. Thus the Revd Moses Davies' claim that the town suffered from Philistinism.

Grimsby has continually been bequeathed the wherewithal for a museum. But it has never been given a building in which to house it. Not that it has been short of suitable buildings which had outgrown their original use, almost all of which have now been demolished. Private individuals of an antiquarian bent made sure that certain civic relics – archaeological finds, military reminders, geological

The Royal Cinema in Grant Street, Cleethorpes opened in October 1921 and, two years later became the Theatre Royal. Versatile and popular it had both cinema screen and capacious stage. These three pictures all taken during a post-war production of *HMS Pinafore* reveal not only the large cast, not only the excellent sets and backdrops but also the packed houses to which Grimsby's troupes were accustomed to play.

specimens and so on – were not discarded and, thanks to them, many 'exhibits' have survived.

The Earl of Yarborough donated maritime paintings and other donors followed suit, notably Edward Bannister. Similar bequests in wills and the like ensured a modest flow of paintings. But these gifts have been accepted with a mix of embarrassment at what to do with them and a 'so-what' shrug of the municipal shoulders.

Matters of this sort, in the minutes of council committees, were given an imperative jolt in the early years of World War Two when Wilfrid Doughty died. Doughty, the only son of Sir George, had been an assiduous collector of nautical things, notably paintings and ship models, all of them of great relevance to the essentially sea-dependent Grimsby.

Although married, Doughty was childless and having parted with his interests in both trawling and the *Grimsby Daily Telegraph* of which at one time he had been editor-proprietor, had become a wealthy man and gone to live far away at Ickfield Manor near Hitchin.

He died in 1941, a week after his 61st birthday, and left his home town the entire collection – the Doughty Bequest – currently valued at about £1million. It arrived, during the war-time blackout, in pantechnicons and, for a town at war, was an awkward import. Hurriedly and variously housed, some of it was destroyed by enemy action and the remainder found a post-war billet in the old grammar school building near the Town Hall. They were cramped quarters for such munificence and, in good time, they were moved again to the empty Congregational chapel in Hainton Avenue.

Currently, the best of the collection is properly exhibited by the side of the old Alexandra Dock. One is bound to ask whether if Grimsby had, like Lincoln and notably Hull, been bequeathed a purpose-built place for its display whether the town could be better off. The answer is, of course, yes. One might say that the Franklin Collection of pictures merely aggravates Grimsby's problem.

But as the town declines, a solution merely recedes. Quiet places of contemplation have never been Grimsby's forte. Grimsby's critics have tried, without success, to give it a polish with which it would certainly have been uncomfortable. Grimsby has not been keen to be hectored.

After the war and during the lean grey days of an austere peace, Grimsby people were generous with their time and devotion in bringing a touch of glamour, and among a host were George Cave, Mary Balders, Eric Boncey and Cecily Bannister.

This line up, from the left: Shirley Waumsley, Sylvia Wringe, Pat Thorndyke, Ann Jolly, Shirley Ashling and Margaret Cooper.

Miss Marie Colebrook's Young Ladies. Left to right: Ann Mcleod, Stephanie Smart, Maxine Skelton, Lesley Green, Marina Hewins and Ann Hayes.

PROVERBS

FAME, said Alexander Pope, comes unlooked for if she comes at all. It was not one of his greatest thoughts. For many court fame and relish it to the full. Grimsby's pedigree has, not surprisingly, resulted in several of its sons and daughters achieving celebrity. But as a rule they had to go elsewhere to find it. And they seldom returned.

Two of its sons have been awarded the Victoria Cross. The first, Lt George Leslie Drewry RN won the award on 25 April 1915 during the frightful disembarkation of troops from the requisitioned collier the ST River Clyde at the Gallipoli landings. His mother was born Mary Ann Kendall and lived at Intax Farm, Weelsby, ultimately off Welholme Road. His father, Thomas, worked in the fitting shops of the MS & L in Grimsby. After a colourful life in the Merchant Service, during which he was wrecked and became a castaway on Hermit Island, Cape Horn, he transferred to the Royal Navy. The citation for his award reveals incredible endeavour. Drewry died as the result of an accident on 3 August 1918 at Scapa Flow.

Grimsby's second Victoria Cross was awarded to Pte Samuel Needham, late of Earl Street, Grimsby, who worked on the Brocklesby Estates and who enlisted in the Bedfordshire Regiment in Hull. One of his sisters was Sir Alec Black's housekeeper. Needham was awarded his Cross at Kair Kasim, Palestine in 1918. But he too was killed accidentally, in November 1918 as he prepared to sail for home. His sister received the award posthumously in Hull.

The stage has provided Grimsby with much

Lt George Leslie Drewry VC, who won the country's highest gallantry honour during the Gallipoli landings in 1915.

reflected glory. Mr and Mrs William Robertson, itinerant actors, were among a troupe visiting Grimsby in 1848, playing the town's first public theatre, a makeshift affair near the ropery works at Riby Square. They took lodgings in the Royal Dock

Pte Samuel Needham VC, whose award came in Palestine in 1918.

destiny was the army. But he became, instead, the greatest of all the Victorian and Edwardian theatrical impressarios, a Grade or Delfont of his illustrious London West End day. Via the Gaiety Theatre, George Edwardes, fluent in French, courteous and gracious, 'a gentleman to his finger tips' said a contemporary, became the confidant of Royalty. His rise to fame was phenomenal. His name became a by-word in play-going.

His other passion was horse-racing and he ran a large racing stable at Ogbourne, Wiltshire, winning both the Ascot Gold Cup and the Cesarawitch. His end was sad. In 1914, and in failing health, he went to Bad Neuheim, Germany to 'take the waters' and was there when war broke out and was interned. As he was suffering from a weak heart, the American consul arranged his release and he came home in October 1914. He died the following year and his theatres closed for a week as a mark of respect. He never forgot his local links and Grimsby friends from long before were treated to the best seats in the

tea and coffee rooms at the Railway Street, Cleethorpe Road corner. And there, on 15 March 1858 Mrs Robertson's 22nd child was born and christened Margaret. She became known in maturity, and having married, as Dame Madge Kendal, and was a celebrated Victorian and Edwardian actress. She was an infrequent visitor to her place of birth. In 1887 the premises in which she was born were sold and demolished and Hewitts the brewers, who had bought it, built the Railway Hotel on the site. After the war and at the instigation of Dorothy Clapham, a plaque was affixed to the hotel wall commemorating Madge Kendal's birth. It was to be the only such plaque ever put up in Grimsby.

Quite the most famous of all Grimbarians – and equally the least well known – was George Edwardes, born at Old Clee in 1852, the son of Captain James Edwardes of the artillery volunteers, Collector of Customs and Receiver of Wrecks, a huge man, 6ft 3ins, Irish and staunchly Roman Catholic. The youngest of five boys (and two sisters) George's

A caricature of George Edwardes – The Guv'nor.

Miss Violet Farebrother pictured in 1960. She was a star of the London stage before and after World War Two.

Freddie Frinton, most famous for his 'drunk' act.

house. At this distance in time the name of George Edwardes is known only to a few.

In his wake there have been several others. Barely recalled is Violet Farebrother (1885–1969) who, in her heyday, was a pre- and post-war star of the London stage who, later, made many television appearances, retiring after 60 years in the profession. Her father, E. W. Farebrother, whose premature death at 35 was a blow to the town, was Grimsby's first celebrated architect, responsible for the Prince of Wales Theatre, the artillery barracks, Scartho workhouse and so on, including many schools. Her mother was a member of the Sutcliffe family. She was a frequent visitor to the town and a patron of the town's amateur Caxton Players.

Freddie Frinton (1915–1968) was from a different mould entirely. The son of Grimsby fisherman, he had a natural aptitude to amuse, was encouraged to do so and became one of the last of the great and

memorable music-hall acts... his 'drunk' act still recalled. In particular because, unusually enough, he became a hero of the German nation and a one-reel short he made with May Walden, entitled *Dinner for One*, is shown without fail every New Year's Eve on German television. In it he plays butler to the elderly May at a dinner party for the deceased... their places being set and Frinton having to 'act' the parts of the vanished guests. In his portrayal of Mr Winterbottom (one of the four absent friends) you will hear the Grimsby accent in all its untamed strength, probably the only occasion it has been given rein on the silver screen. Freddie Frinton also did not forget his home town and despite great fame, particularly with co-star Thora Hird in the TV series *Meet The Wife*, was a regular visitor and contributor to the life of his birthplace.

Television was also the vehicle for Patrick Wymark (1926–1970) born in Grimsby as Patrick Cheeseman. Although he made, in his short life, several films, notably *Where Eagles Dare* and, in 1969, *Cromwell*, it was on television and in the two

Patrick Wymark, a household name through his television roles..

Actress Patricia Hodge, daughter of the licensees of the Royal Hotel.

Former world motor-cycle champion Freddie Frith.

series *The Plane Makers* and *The Power Game* – in which latter he played the part of a tycoon – that he became a household name.

Heir to all these turns and thespians is Patricia Hodge, daughter of the licensees of the Royal Hotel, now demolished and once just across the road from the old Railway Hotel. Miss Hodge, too, is an occasional visitor to her hometown.

The sporting life has brought much fame. Foremost among its recipients was Freddie Frith (1910–1988), the son of a celebrated stonemason and domestic sculptor whose work survives in many local houses. Trained in the job like his father before him, Freddie Frith found fulfilment on motorcycles, was four times Isle of Man Tourist Trophy winner and, in 1949 became the World Motorcycle champion...when he retired. He never left Grimsby

Wedding day for Shirley Bloomer and Olympic gold medalist Chris Brasher in 1959.

and was later in the motor cycle business in the town. Wimbledon was the stage for Shirley Bloomer's success. The granddaughter of the solicitor Howard Kossuth Bloomer (1860–1930), she became British, Italian and French hardcourt tennis champion and was seeded number-one at Wimbledon in the 1950s. She later married the Olympic gold medallist athlete Christopher Brasher.

Until 1935 Haydn Taylor (1897–1962) was just a local dentist. That year his swimming of the English Channel made him celebrated. But his fame was nothing like that of Miss Brenda Fisher, born in Grimsby in 1928 and who, in 1951, swam the Channel in 12 hours 42 minutes establishing a new women's record. She returned from her victory to thunderous civic applause and a reception in the town never accorded an individual since.

It is said that the peculiar hours kept by Grimsby fishermen was contributory to the popularity in the town of billiards and snooker halls. Whether true or not, the town has certainly produced some very good exponents of both games. The name of Ray Edmonds is to be found in the lists of past masters for he became World Amateur Billiards champion.

Horse racing has, maybe second-hand – for it is surely the horse which is the victor – brought passing glory. In the 19th century the Marshalls, millers and timber importers all, owned famous horses and William Robinson Marshall (1836–1904) owned the Grand Prix de Paris winner, won the

Brenda Fisher, who in 1951 established a new women's record for swimming the Channel.

Sir David Plastow, a managing director and chief executive of Rolls-Royce Motors, and chairman of Vickers. His background was steeped in Grimsby's history.

Goodwood Cup and had horses placed in the St Leger and the 1899 Derby. The great fishing magnate Sir Alec Black (1872–1942) far outstripped this modest tally. He was 44 when he first took an interest and in the ensuing 20 years won the 2,000 Guineas in 1919 with The Panther. Later he won the St Leger with Singapore, the 2,000 Guineas with Colombo and the 1,000 Guineas with Brown Betty.

The world of commerce has shown Grimsby men not to be backward, and surely the wealthiest man ever to have been born in Grimsby was William Weightman, a butcher's apprentice when he left the town, who died in Philadelphia in August 1904, aged 90. He had a bent for pharmacy and went, penniless, in pursuit of an uncle to Philadelphia, devoting his life to chemistry and, in particular – to quinine manufacture. Briefly, his company became the greatest maker of the drug and, at his death he was immensely rich, his fortune estimated at £120 million dollars, more than £10 million sterling.

Sir Joseph Nickerson, knighted by a grateful country and grandson of a Grimsby smack owner, became a larger than life agriculturalist, keeping the company of kings and bringing to his native North Lincolnshire fame, fortune, employment and devotion.

Frank Smith (1877–1966) erudite artesian well expert, who invented 'expanded piling' which became a boon to construction work, must be numbered in this list. The Globe Cinema in Victoria Street was the first building to be constructed on this principal. The Expanded Piling Company's rights were sold in 1991 for £21 million.

The Globe Cinema, pictured around 1930.

No one becomes managing director and chief executive of Rolls-Royce Motors by accident and such was the success of David Plastow, later knighted, who retired as chairman of Vickers in 1992. Sir David's background was entirely Grimsby's, his forebears smack owners, his grandfather chairman of Grimsby Town Football Club.

The world of letters has touched Grimsby but lightly. Ivy Wallace was the daughter of Dr William Wallace (1874–1947) whose practice was at Hainton Square. His brother was the once celebrated Berwick artist James Wallace. Ivy, an animal lover and wartime secretary to the chief constable, Charles Butler, wrote the post-war series of children's treats the Pookie Books, best sellers in their day. And she illustrated them too, her artistic skills honed in Grimsby Town Hall in the chief constable's service!

Roy Faiers, whose father Phil Faiers was Freddie Frinton's pianist, is that rare combination of journalist and businessman. Striking out on his own he ultimately founded the national magazine *This England* which enjoys a worldwide circulation.

In the same, but more irreverent, vein Old Harrovian Andrew Osmond who regrettably and prematurely died in 1999 aged 60 was one of the co-founders of the satirical *Private Eye* magazine. His Baptist great-grandfather, Kingsford Venner Osmond (1824–1900), who came to Grimsby in 1869 as a New Clee schoolmaster, planted the first tree in Hainton Avenue and his son, Leslie Kingsford Osmond (1864–1946) was mayor of Grimsby in 1926 and a one-time president of Grimsby Town FC. The Osmond stand is named after him.

John Brown (1887–1975), grandson of his namesake who built Grimsby in its Victorian heyday, became an expert bridge player and subsequently

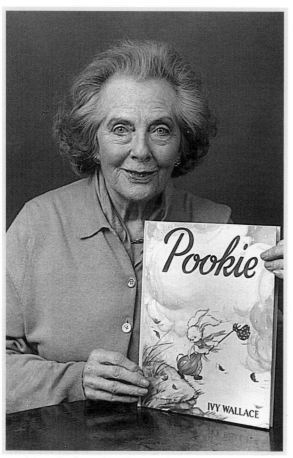

Ivy Wallace, pictured with one of her Pookie books.

wrote *Winning Tricks*, a standard on many a bridge player's bookshelf. John Brown jnr was a typical third generation Grimbarian with a background of The Leys, Cambridge and Sidney Sussex. He was also an accomplished artist.

In the pages of *Benezit* you will find Thomas Benjamin Kennington (1856–1916) the Grimsby-born artist whose portrait of Edward Bannister is so memorable and, indeed that of his son Eric Kennington (1888–1947) internationally celebrated, the latter immediately associated with the superb portrait of T.E. Lawrence. Both Kenningtons exhibited at the Tate.

A miscellany of the famous must include Tom Wintringham (1898–1949) who commanded the English battalion of the International Brigade during the Spanish Civil War, was several times wounded and acclaimed a hero. A member of the Communist Party until his expulsion from it in 1938 he was the second son of John Fildes Wintringham (1866–1940) senior partner of Grange and Wintringham, Borough Registrar, and one of the town's most outstanding sportsmen. Tom Wintringham, whose brother was Colonel J.W. Wintringham of the Yeomanry was an author, RAF despatch rider, an ex-Balliol man who twice stood for Parliament (for the Commonwealth Party) and was twice unelected.

Otto Overbeck (1860–1937), the Grimsby brewer, was initially well known after inventing a jiggery-pokery 'rejuvenator' which attempted to produce vim and vigour by self-administered electrical impulses. Some survive (the rejuvenators, that is). He achieved more fame when he presented his considerable estate – Sharpitor at Salcombe in Devon – to the National Trust. It is his memorial.

Patrick Cormack, son of Thomas Charles Cormack (1910–1977) became locally celebrated as the first Havelock schoolboy (Carr Lane) to go to university, and then was elected MP for Cannock, Staffordshire in 1970. He was knighted in 1994.

Vivian Hewitt, nephew of the well-known Grimsby millionaire brewer T.W.G. Hewitt was, in 1912, the first man to fly across the Irish Sea.

Sixth Officer James P. Moody was on the bridge of the *Titanic* when she struck the iceberg in 1912 – and is commemorated in St Augustine's Church, Grimsby. He was drowned attempting, with others, to launch a lifeboat. His grandfather. Dr C.B. Moody (1815–1895) was the first Grimsby coroner (1891).

Mr J. Carl Ross, to whom in no small part Grimsby owes much of its current prosperity, was the last of the great fishing moguls, a giant in the land of fishing giants, his surname still household in the country's supermarkets. His father, Thomas, was a Yorkshire Wesleyan who came here in the thriving years (1885) aged 15 and, after 10 years' employment with Thomas Robinson, set up in business on the pontoon as a fish merchant.

A brilliant local preacher – 'a man of prayer' who knew his bible by heart – he miraculously survived the Barnetby rail disaster and gave away the

J. Carl Ross (left). The last of the great fishing moguls, his surname is still household in the country's supermarkets. He is pictured here with Tory minister McLeod (centre) and Alderman Denys Petchell.

compensation he received after it. His escape, he said, was 'God's will'. He had settled in Cleethorpes where he named his home Filey House in deference to his origins.

His son, Carl, a daring innovator who learned particularly from his Gamaliel and close friend Sir Alec Black, realised in the middle of a successful business career that it was frozen food which held the key to a future. When he had taken over his father's firm at the age of 28 he had 34 employees. When he retired he employed 15,000. He had taken over many celebrated trawling firms and he and his partner Jack Vincent built what became known as the Ross Group (of companies) which were to keep Grimsby on the map and to survive the demise of the visible trawling industry.

THE EPILOGUE

THIS is not an obituary. Towns do not die. They may change, decline, prosper, vegetate. They do not perish. Grimsby has changed. But it shows no sign of keeling over. For a town is not merely a collection of buildings. A town is the people who live in it. And coursing through the veins of those who live in it yet is the resolve of those who came here 150 years ago to make it one of the most vibrant places in the kingdom.

We may look back – indeed we do, for nostalgia has ever been the escape of the English – to the 'good old days' and remember sights and sounds and smells which are no longer. But Grimsby has never had time to make reminiscence its master. And a good thing too. For adaptation has always been the keynote to his continuing success.

In matters of commerce the south bank of the Humber is a beacon for England at present. Grimsby is surely its brightest flame. Years ago, at midnight of a New Year's Eve, Grimsby people would go to their doors, step out into the starry night and listen with pride and confirmation of their town's standing as the trawlers blew their sirens in the Humber.

This year, as in many past, the silence is only gently disturbed. But what did we expect from 2002? Not, surely in the age of the computer the rattle of the typewriter. Such things are gone. But not the spirit of them. In 1800 when Grimsby reached its nadir, no one could possibly have foretold the tide of industry that was to overwhelm it, transform it into the greatest fishing port in the world... and there has never been a greater.

In 1900 no one could foretell its fate. The town appeared to be at an unassailable zenith... as indeed did the British Empire to which Grimsby added its own lustre. But all things change... all things.

The Rockies may crumble, Gibraltar may tumble as the song has it. But... There is always a 'but'. The past is only sad if one allows it to be so.

The past, in fact, supplies a source of strength, not regret. It provides an example, an example not to copy but to better. Grimsby is, as it was, a splendid town entirely because of the people who used to live in it and those who do so presently. We are proud of a determined past. But it is not the pride which comes before a fall.

Bargate is Grimsby's southern approach and it and its immediate surroundings do, miraculously, survive and are afforded some sort of conservation area protection. This view, revealing a road surface wreathed in tram lines is variously recognisable. A coal cart from Edward Bannister's firm wends its way back to town (centre).

Herbert Rollett, Grimsby grocer, is recalled for his prowess with oil paint and canvas. But he was also a competent photographer, this view of Abbey Road, with Clarence Terrace (Spectacle Terrace) in the distance revealing an Edwardian calm.

By the happiest of coincidences when the photographer pressed his camera button, one day in 1938, he just happened to capture – in this view of the old cottages on Bargate – these two people on their rounds. They were Effie Winifred Lewis and Frederick Anselm Parker, representatives both of the Britannic Assurance Company who, for a lifetime combined commerce and an undying love for each other. But although Effie was a spinster, Fred was married. They conducted their most proper 'affair' by means of letters, postcards and, most of all, gifts of books all lovingly inscribed. Released by death from his loveless bond, Fred finally married Effie at Old Clee in 1951, she 68, he 77. Two years later he died. She died in 1968 aged 83. Grimsby has no love story like it.

This area of town includes some first class villas and houses. But, of the buildings in the neighbourhood, none matches the importance of the former County Magistrates' Court in Brighowgate, the work of the architect Herbert Scaping, a delightful Edwardian Arts and Crafts tour de force, the future of which hangs, at the time of writing, in the balance.

Harold Hillam (1906-81), the Grimsby schoolmaster who took many of the photographers in this book.

INDEX